MW00345151

The GROWING Points Star

A Tool for Disciple Formation

DUANE M GEBHARD

DISCIPLESHIP RESOURCES

P.O. BOX 340003 • NASHVILLE, TN 37203-0003
www.discipleshipresources.org

Cover design by Sharon Anderson

Book design by Nanci Lamar

ISBN 0-88177-302-6

Library of Congress Catalog Card No. 99-65955

Scripture quotations, unless otherwise indicated, are from the New Revised Standard Version of the Bible, copyright © 1989 by the Division of Christian Education of the National Council of the Churches of Christ in the USA. All rights reserved. Used by permission.

THE GROWING POINTS STAR: A Tool of Disciple Formation. Copyright © 2000 Discipleship Resources. All rights reserved. No part of this book may be reproduced in any form whatsoever, print or electronic, without written permission, except in the case of brief quotations embodied in critical articles or reviews. Pages labeled as reproducible may be photocopied by the purchaser for use with this book. For information regarding rights and permissions, contact Discipleship Resources Editorial Offices, P.O. Box 340003, Nashville, TN 37203-0003, phone 615-340-7068, fax 615-340-1789, e-mail mgregory@gbod.org.

DR302

Contents

773-310-4647

of the nineteenth century to DISCIPLE Bible study of recent times, from "alive" worship in the Wesleyan spirit to gatherings around the campfire, and on and on—the elements discussed in this book occur with varying degrees of effectiveness. The issue is to give careful attention to assure that all of these essential elements are present, in order to more consistently assist people to grow in faith and discipleship.

MEANS OF GRACE

John Wesley identified certain spiritual disciplines or practices as means of grace. He believed that as a person practices the means of grace regularly, he or she experiences a growing awareness of God's love and grace. For Wesley, these means of grace included worship, daily prayer, the study of Scripture, the Lord's Supper, fasting or abstinence, Christian conferencing or conversation, and acts of mercy. The means of grace practiced by Wesley undergird all five of the growing points, provide a means by which one continues to grow in discipleship, and assist in faith formation for others.

THE GROWING POINTS STAR AS A TOOL FOR DISCIPLE FORMATION

The Growing Points Star grew out of the conviction that as we pay careful attention to the conditions, the relationships, and the basic concepts that surround each of the growing points, we can more consistently and effectively help people come to know Jesus Christ and step into the flowing stream of God's Spirit and grace.

A remarkable growing edge throughout the Christian movement around the world is that more and more people are seeking to live their whole lives, day in and day out, in a way that is consistent with the gospel of Jesus Christ. The Growing Points Star is a way to pay attention more consistently to the elements that contribute to faith formation and growth as a disciple of Christ.

USING THE GROWING POINTS STAR IN THE LOCAL CHURCH

The Growing Points Star is a powerful tool for learning about aspects that influence one's entry into faith in Jesus Christ. The concepts in this book—beginning with reflection on one's personal journey, moving on to teach others about the growing points, then using the Growing Points Star as a tool to develop practices that contribute to the developing faith of others—are a unique backdrop for effective disciple formation.

The Growing Points Star is an effective tool for
- understanding and teaching about factors that influence growth in the faith;
- helping us think critically about how our actions help or hinder others as they come to know Christ;
- helping to identify constraints in your church's system of disciple formation;
- encouraging new ideas that facilitate growth in the faith;
- evaluating the effectiveness of worship and preaching;
- planning faith-forming experiences;
- training spiritual leaders (lay and clergy) in key factors that influence faith development;
- training camp leaders in key factors that influence faith development.

All who believed were together and had all things in common... Day by day, as they spent much time together in the temple, they broke bread at home and ate their food with glad and generous hearts, praising God and having the goodwill of all the people. And day by day the Lord added to their number those who were being saved.

(Acts 2:44, 46-47)

Paying attention to the elements identified in the growing points helps people move in their faith journey from floundering helplessly in the chaos of life to swimming joyfully in the flowing currents of God's life-giving Spirit. The growing points, with Jesus Christ at the center, draw attention and focus to our primary task of forming faithful disciples.

ANTICIPATED OUTCOMES OF USING THE GROWING POINTS STAR

As the insights from the growing points are put into practice, the following outcomes will be experienced:
- greater focus on our mission of making disciples for Jesus Christ;
- clarity of the meaning of discipleship;
- understanding about factors that influence growth in the faith;
- joy in more creatively and effectively sharing our faith in Jesus Christ;
- meaning-making as people discover their own stories in the context of God's story;
- people on the shore of experience in the faith being drawn into the mainstream of God's flowing Spirit;
- the power and presence of the Holy Spirit experienced in all aspects of church life;
- regular practice of the means of grace by more disciples;
- new entry points identified for those coming to and growing in faith.

When we, as spiritual leaders, live with an awareness of the growing points that contribute to a developing faith in Christ, we can become coaches on whom others can depend as they take the first steps into the stream of God's Spirit and grace. To be more capable coaches for those learning to swim in the current of growing faith, spiritual leaders must be familiar with and able to use comfortably the elements that contribute to developing relationships with Jesus Christ and living as faithful disciples.

We will find as we help others that the Spirit of Christ continues to grow stronger at the center of our lives, individually and in community, so that we can proclaim with Paul: "It is no longer I who live, but it is Christ who lives in me" (Galatians 2:20). Our communities of faith can become known to us not only as church but also as the living body of Christ.

Chapter Two

Growing Point One:

I Hear My Name

Beginning relationship

On the last day of the festival, the great day, while Jesus was standing there, he cried out, "Let anyone who is thirsty come to me, and let the one who believes in me drink. As the scripture has said, 'Out of the believer's heart shall flow rivers of living water.'"

(John 7:37-38)

Discovering Jesus Christ, growing in the faith, and living as a disciple of Christ is a process that continues throughout one's lifetime. The first growing point, beginning relationship, calls our attention to factors that contribute to new beginnings along the journey of a developing faith. That journey often starts as one experiences the gentle touch of Christ's love through the acts of care and compassion of another person.

One's personal openness and receptivity to the Spirit of Christ is influenced by various factors, which may include personal experiences, the surrounding environment, and the actions of other people. Internal factors such as an individual's longing for God may increase one's openness, while other internal factors such as negative religious experiences may be barriers to overcome. Whatever our situation, the Spirit of Christ can always be counted on to be present and active in our lives.

The application questions in this book may be used as a guide for personal reflection, or they could be used in a group setting as a basis for discussion and further study.

Application Questions

1. Think back over the past several weeks. Can you recall a time when someone reached out to you with the gentle touch of Christ's love? What did it feel like?

2. In your church, what group (ministry team, committee, or ad hoc group) takes responsibility for reaching out to new people in caring and respectful ways?

3. Imagine yourself as a first-time visitor to your church or group. What would the first conversations and relationships feel like?

4. How does your congregation reach out beyond its walls to call people by name?

Because relationships and community help a person feel accepted and valued by God and by other people, they are powerful support as one begins to grow in the faith. As people come to new faith in Jesus Christ, it is necessary to pay attention to those dynamics that contribute to beginning relationships. Every relationship has a beginning, and a new experience or relationship with Jesus Christ is no different. The relationship frequently is influenced by others and the way they relate to us. We often are unaware of how critical initial encounters are. People must bring their own thoughts, emotions, and life experiences to a newly emerging awareness of God's love and acceptance, which is made known by others sharing the love of Christ by reaching out with acts of kindness and understanding.

Theresa recalled that her deep faith in Christ grew bit by bit through her childhood as she attended camps led by her parents. As the youth groups were guided through campfire experiences, led in discussions and songs of the faith, taken with mission work teams to carry out service and acts of love for others, and encouraged to consider commitment to Christ, Theresa grew in her relationship with Christ. It is no surprise, then, that as she considered the elements or conditions that contributed to her growth in the faith, she identified those that she had experienced in camp and retreat settings. She had felt valued and accepted as she was because her contributions and stories were acknowledged by others, and she had learned to trust the presence of a spirit of love and caring that she later came to know as the love of Jesus Christ.

KEY FACTORS IN A BEGINNING RELATIONSHIP

Imbedded in my childhood memories is an encounter with a man my mother affectionately referred to as Prexy Brown. Periodically, our family visited his family at their summer retreat in Michigan. I was a child of only eight or nine, but for some reason Dr. Brown, who had been the president of the college Mother had attended, asked me to go on a walk with him. During the walk, he showed great interest in me, wanting to know what I thought about, what I was learning, and what I would like my life to become. I often wondered why he cared so much about me. His caring made a deep impression on me, and for years I tried to live up to the faith he showed in me. Later, I thought that he was truly a living example of what Jesus Christ would be. When I went to Africa as a young adult to be a missionary, Prexy Brown wrote a long letter encouraging me to live daily as a disciple of Christ and offering suggestions as to how I could accomplish that. I was truly led into God's presence by Prexy Brown's acceptance, love, and faith in God through Jesus Christ.

Others have similar experiences that help shape their faith in Jesus Christ and trust in God. Two close friends first met on a running track during the lunch break at a conference. As they ran around the track on that hot summer day, their conversation led them to discover that they each recently had experienced a painful time. They reached out to each other in acceptance and understanding, forming a bond that has brought healing and joy to them over the years. They felt reassured as children of God to go on with their lives, faithfully trusting in the presence of Christ they felt in each other.

Such is the case in our relationship with Jesus Christ. We have beginning moments, when we become more and more aware of a spirit of acceptance and reassurance expressed by those around us. At first we may not be able to describe what is happening; however, we gradually sense that we are valued just as we are. But there is more. It is as if we are being introduced to a spirit of love and caring that runs even more deeply than the friendship or love that is possible between two people. We are beginning to experience what we may later come to know as the gentle touch of Christ's love. Although we may not recognize it at the time, it is as though we are just dipping our toes into that stream that becomes the powerful flow of the Holy Spirit through our lives.

I Hear My Name

This feeling of acceptance grows stronger as we sense that someone else knows and calls us by name. Our names are vitally important, as they represent who we are and define our identity. "The LORD called me before I was born, while I was in my mother's womb he named me," says Isaiah in affirmation of God's knowledge of each person as a special and unique individual (Isaiah 49:1b). "[The shepherd] calls his own sheep by name and leads them out," assures Jesus (John 10:3b). Yet, for people who do not know Christ or the promises he makes, the assurance by other people that they are valued and accepted reaches deep into their souls. Often, this happens as we hear our name spoken respectfully by another.

A woman whose family had ridiculed and isolated her from others when she was a child and youth was invited to participate in a small group for support and study. As the sessions went by, she gradually felt a kind of acceptance she had never known. After a guided meditation at one session, she reported to the group the powerful image that had come to her: She was standing at the foot of the steps of a large airplane where passengers were disembarking. As relatives who had ignored or mistreated her came off the airplane, they each greeted her and lovingly called her by name. She said that being reassured of the presence of Christ allowed her to be open to hearing her name on the lips of those who had mistreated her.

The beginning relationship in Christ happens as one who has not experienced the presence of Christ receives and accepts the outpouring of love expressed by another person living in the awareness of Christ's Spirit. This can happen at any age and at any time. It may happen so subtly that we do not recognize what is taking place; we simply feel accepted, valued, and known by name.

Gentle and Reassuring Presence

Beth heard that her neighbor had just received some bad news about a family member. She went next door and said, "We care about you and will keep you in our prayers. I just want to assure you that God will be with you through this. I'll bring dinner over tonight and watch the children, if you would like." The neighbor, who was not aware of Christ's presence in her own life and had little time for the church, sensed that what was being expressed was much more than friendliness. Beth represented trust in a spiritual power that transcended life. Beth's neighbor felt assured that through Beth's prayers and concern, she would be cared for not only by her friend but also by God. Before long, Beth's neighbor wanted to find out more about this spirit of trust, reassurance, and caring.

A beginning relationship starts as someone who experiences the presence and love of Christ in his or her life reaches out in acceptance and reassurance to

O LORD, you have searched me and known me. You know when I sit down and when I rise up; you discern my thoughts from far away. You search out my path and my lying down, and are acquainted with all my ways. Even before a word is on my tongue, O LORD, you know it completely.... For it was you who formed my inward parts; you knit me together in my mother's womb. I praise you, for I am fearfully and wonderfully made. Wonderful are your works; that I know very well. (Psalm 139:1-4, 13-14)

15

Application Questions

1. How did Beth's actions and words express the gentle touch of Christ's love?

2. Identify several ways in which youth in your church or community can be helped to experience the love of Christ through the actions of other people. How might they respond?

someone else. Perhaps it happens at a time of particular vulnerability, when that person is especially receptive to the realization that someone cares. Maybe it happens during a time of growth and awareness of new things, or when simply responding to the deep human longing to be known and valued by another person and by God. What makes the caring unique is that the person feels accepted and valued, regardless of the situation. That person begins to think, *If another person could care this much, maybe God could care too.*

As we go through life, we experience this reaching out by others in a variety of ways. Children between the ages of five and ten are especially receptive to the rituals and practices of the faith that are important to their parents and other adults in the church. These rituals and practices become important in their lives even before they understand them. For example, children love to watch closely as an infant is being baptized, although they may not fully understand the meaning of the ritual. They also enjoy taking part in the Lord's Supper because they have learned that it is an important ritual in our faith. Children do not necessarily understand the symbolism behind the rituals; however, their understanding changes as they mature.

Most churches need to be more sensitive to the age-specific needs of children and youth as they discover the Spirit of Christ. Paying attention to beginning relationships for children and youth will contribute greatly to their growth in the faith. Pastors and other worship leaders must engage children and youth in ways that reflect sensitivity to their individuality and stage in life. Likewise, adults at various ages and stages in life need to be responded to in ways that are respectful of who they are. For example, older adults living in healthcare facilities love to be prompted with the question "Would you like to tell me some of your favorite memories in the church?"

I FEEL ACCEPTED AND VALUED BY OTHERS AND BY GOD

Jesus frequently interacted with people who were otherwise rejected by the rest of society. He brought them into the center of peoples' attention and ministered to their needs. One example after another can be named: Jesus beckoning the children to come to him (Matthew 19:14), the Canaanite woman whose daughter was tormented by a demon (Matthew 15:22), the woman caught in sin who was about to be stoned (John 8:4), the man with a withered hand whom Jesus healed on a sabbath (Matthew 12:10), the Gerasene demoniac from whom Jesus cast the evil spirits into the heard of swine (Mark 5), the blind man at Bethsaida (Mark 8:22), the tax collector Zacchaeus (Luke 19:1-10), the woman at the well in Samaria (John 4), and others. Jesus valued each of these people and let them know it, and he often called them by name. Frequently, he asked them to talk about what they were seeking.

In the Great Commission, Jesus made it abundantly clear that the Spirit of Christ wants to work through us to meet people at the point of their need and to minister to them: "Go therefore and make disciples of all nations, baptizing them in the name of the Father and of the Son and of the Holy Spirit, and teaching them to obey everything that I have commanded you. And remember, I am with you always, to the end of the age" (Matthew 28:19-20).

In a beginning relationship, a person must be accepted and valued as a person so that Christ can be known. It is far more than hospitality as we understand it. This acceptance may be expressed by telling another person how one has experienced the presence of Jesus Christ or what has been learned about his teachings. The name of Jesus may not even be mentioned. However, we always leave the matter of changing another person's heart up to God, for we cannot give the Spirit of Christ to another person. Only Christ can do that, and he will. What we can give is our own love, based on what we have experienced of Christ's love in our own life. We can accept one another through that love; we can show what that love can do; and we can trust in that love for ourselves. God works through our words and actions to assure others that they are loved and accepted by God. The gentle touch of Christ's love is expressed and felt by all involved in the beginning relationship as people live the love of Christ that they have experienced. The beginning relationship is about reaching out to meet the Christ who is already in another person and letting Christ be part of the new relationship that develops as a result of the encounter.

We never know when or how Christ will work through us to heal, but we can help others recognize Christ's love and respond to it. After a healing service during a workshop on developing skills in spiritual leadership for pastors, one pastor said, "Christ was so real that I felt as if he touched me with the hand of healing for the first time in my life!"

Helping Someone Awaken to the Spirit of Christ

When one approaches another in the Spirit of Christ, there is, often in spite of the words or actions that are used, a Christ-like encounter, similar to the way Jesus related to people on the streets and in the countryside of Galilee. People have a consciousness of unrealized desires to know God and be known by God. When the woman at the well in Samaria realized that Jesus was the Messiah, she was so overjoyed that she ran to tell her friends so that they, too, could come meet him (John 4:28-29). When will our faith in Christ be so joy-filled that we cannot wait for new opportunities to help others experience beginning relationships that lead to new faith in Christ?

The beginning relationship is an essential growing point because it is a first "hello" to God. It is the invitation to venture into the waters of faith that allows one to experience the full flow of God's Spirit for the first time, or in a way that leads to a greater depth of faith in Jesus Christ. It is saying "hello" to a new beginning.

Sometimes the beginning relationship may be a powerful experience that leads to complete transformation at the center of one's life. It has such an impact that the person has a totally new outlook on life—a new attitude toward everything and everybody, including one's relationship with God. Whether one is taking a small incremental step toward deeper faith or is experiencing complete transformation, the soul that is coming alive in Christ needs careful nurturing and involvement in the other aspects of the faith, which are identified in the other growing points.

Conditions of the Beginning Relationship

Most people in love can recall easily the details of the first time they met: the song that became special, the place that stands out in memory, or a food that has become a favorite. These conditions contribute to the ambience of the setting and help form the memory of the event, but they are less important than the relationship that began to develop at that time and place.

Application Questions

1. Discuss in your group (or record your own thoughts about) ways to recognize Christ in another person.

2. What kinds of action or nonverbal communication help someone know that he or she is valued and loved by God?

Application Questions

1. How can we be more sensitive to the needs of other people as they say "hello" to God's Spirit?

2. What factors contribute to creating a welcoming environment for one who is looking for God?

Application Questions

1. Think carefully about the times in your own life when you grew quickly in your faith. What conditions contributed to your growth? What role did other people play in that growth?

2. Find others who seem to be living out of a strong faith in Christ. Invite them to tell about the conditions that were present for them at the beginning of the relationship and the role played by other people.

3. Use personal examples as you tell about the importance of the factors and conditions surrounding the beginning of the relationship.

As people of faith, we must pay attention to the conditions surrounding the opportunities for this growing point in the lives of other people, even though the conditions play a secondary role. The place where the relationship begins often becomes special, not because of its uniqueness but because of what happened there. The other people who were there at the time often are remembered, because they help identify what happened when the relationship began. Other conditions such as music, food, smells, and even the weather may have set the stage in which the relationship began. Though these conditions are contributing factors that may help form memories that recall an event or setting, what is most important is that a beginning relationship with Christ developed because something happened between people in the presence of Christ.

A Final Note

Sometimes the recipient strongly resists the Spirit of Christ. Like early morning fog that refuses to be burned off by the rising sun, the resistance of a closed mind, prejudice, old tapes, or negative memories is like a cloud that will never lift. With perseverance and the powerful love of Christ, the fog will burn away and dissipate into thin air. Then one will be open to the encouragement of others and take the first steps leading into the new stream of faith that is beginning its long journey to the sea.

As we help others begin a new relationship, we may experience new growth in our own faith and in our own awareness of the Spirit of Christ.

Chapter Three

Growing Point Two:

I Belong Here

Beginning relationship

Experiencing Christian community

Then little children were being bought to him in order that he might lay his hands on them and pray. The disciples spoke sternly to those who brought them; but Jesus said, "Let the little children come to me, and do not stop them; for it is to such as these that the kingdom of heaven belongs." (Matthew 19:13-14)

Jesus frequently helped people feel a sense of welcome and acceptance. They felt this not only in his presence but also in his admonishment of the judgment, rejection, and cold shoulders sometimes given by his disciples and other followers. As the disciples tried to send the children away, Jesus said, "Let the little children come to me, and do not stop them" (Matthew 19:14). When the Pharisees threatened a woman caught in adultery, Jesus said, "Let anyone among you who is without sin be the first to throw a stone at her" (John 8:7). Again and again Jesus established the worth of individuals and drew them into relationship with others.

Jesus was responding to one of the deepest longings of human beings: the experience of community without ridicule, judgment, or condemnation. How do we know about this need? If you observe any school playground at recess, you will see that most of the children are gathered in groups. They are not standing or playing alone, each one seemingly oblivious to the others. Of those who are alone, many long to be included in some group and, if invited, would run to join—that is, unless they have already experienced rejection or ridicule or have been bruised by interacting with others. Protective instincts often produce a reluctance to interact further with a group.

Another indicator of the desire for community is what happens in many churches following a service of worship: People gather in a reception area or fellowship hall for coffee, refreshments, and fellowship. Friends usually gather in small groups to visit. Some enjoy going from group to group, mixing gracefully. Invariably, new people find it much more difficult to break into conversation groups and feel comfortable. (*New* in some communities means that the person has arrived more recently than fifteen or even twenty years ago.) Occasionally, perceptive individuals look for those who would appreciate an invitation to join the group. Some people are learning the importance of having greater sensitivity toward visitors.

A true sign of our longing for community is the feeling we get when we are not able to enter groups that are already formed. Our emotions may range from disappointment to deep hurt. We leave a gathering such as a fellowship time after worship with little desire to return. When we think about our feelings, we discover that our basic longing to experience community has not been met.

Certainly, there are loners who are happier by themselves than with others. In fact, all of us occasionally need time alone. Nevertheless, we seek community that is nonthreatening and accepting of us just as we are, without perceived judgment. We respond willingly and openly to a community that moves beyond one-to-one relationships and draws us into a gathering where spiritual unity is felt. The apostle Paul refers to "the unity of the Spirit in the bond of peace," acknowledging that the Spirit of Christ draws us together as we experience gentleness, humility, patience, and a "bearing with one another in love" (Ephesians 4:2-3).

One definition of *Christian community* might be "a group or fellowship of people with the common interest of exchanging ideas, thoughts, and experiences of the Christian faith." This definition adequately covers what many people experience within the church community; however, it falls far short of describing what truly happens as community is formed with a conscious awareness that Christ is present.

The second growing point, experiencing Christian community, focuses on discovering a unique and reassuring form of community that happens when each person is accepted and valued and the presence of Christ is acknowledged.

PEOPLE ARE WELCOME JUST AS THEY ARE

A church council that was on retreat for planning and team building was led in a guided meditation so that they could think about the experience visitors have when they come to worship. The participants were asked to imagine moving to a new community and looking for a new church that would be as close to perfect as possible. The leader encouraged them to think through arriving at this imaginary church, being welcomed, worshiping, and then leaving. As they discussed the experience later, most admitted that they had never experienced hospitality as they had imagined or hoped it could be. Why not?

In part, it has to do with turf. Most people look at a new person as a visitor, an outsider. The unspoken attitude is that visitors do not really belong and are just passing through. Thus, visitors must make an effort to discover who we are and fit in by learning how we do things. After all, the rest of us had to go through the same process when we were new, didn't we? With true hospitality, on the other hand, every effort is made to help the invited guest feel welcome and at home. The visitor could be viewed as one who might bring us new insights about Jesus Christ.

Bill, a member of First Church for fifteen years, has served on the administrative board and chaired several committees. While these tasks have helped him meet his sense of obligation as a member of the church, Bill receives his greatest satisfaction from a self-appointed role that he quietly carries out every Sunday morning. He takes special delight in going to the entrance area of the church, looking for at least one new person, and greeting him or her in a warm, caring way. He then draws the new person into conversation with someone else with whom he feels that person might have something in common. Often, a first-time visitor is the recipient of Bill's own private mission, but sometimes it is one of the youth or someone who is also alone. Bill's weekly efforts have led to a deeper experience of community for many people, because newly formed relationships lead to involvement in small groups, the choir, mission teams, or the youth group. Many people recall the time when Bill met them and introduced them to the life of the church. Bill understands the importance not only of the beginning relationship but also of the reassuring welcome of a community in the Spirit of Christ.

A first-time visitor in worship may be seated among total strangers. After a few genuine words of welcome, the worship leader might say, "Let us greet one another in the Spirit of Christ." This simple act says, "You are welcome, and we accept you." It must be accompanied by a corporate worship experience that says, through signs, symbols, words, and actions, "You are valued as a person; we accept you without judgment." The bulletin must be user-friendly for those unfamiliar with the patterns of worship, and the actions of people around the visitor must reflect acceptance and a desire to reach out to welcome someone new. Hospitality demands that we relieve the awkwardness a visitor may be feeling and be respectful of that individual. For example, giving a visitor a hug may make the visitor feel uncomfortable.

When a church community is not respectful of elements that help others feel welcome, the results can be devastating. Some travelers who had stopped at a visitor center on the way into a Midwestern town asked for recommendations for a place to worship. The following Sunday they followed the directions to the church that had been recommended. They were greatly disappointed. The service of worship was fine and the preaching was strong, but the congregation was unfriendly. When they arrived, no one spoke to them or helped them find a place to sit. Later, they heard someone exclaim, "Those people are in our pew." When the service was over, no one spoke to them as they left. On their way out of town, they stopped again at the visitor center and suggested that the host never recommend that church again.

Those of us who have been part of one congregation for a while generally come to accept as normal its unique style of community, warts and all. We are more forgiving of shortcomings in hospitality when acted out by people we have known and accepted for years than we would be if we were newcomers. We do not mind seeing unsightly tables in the entryway or outdated posters on the walls. These elements and others represent serious blind spots that must be corrected if we really want to welcome strangers when they come to visit.

Application Questions

1. How are new people invited to become part of a small group within your congregation? Does the group change its posture and positioning in order to include the new person?

2. Is the person made welcome irrespective of his or her unique characteristics, such as skin color, accent (or language), clothes, or demeanor? List two or three factors that make welcome possible.

3. Is the person included in the conversation in a respectful way so that he or she knows this is a safe environment?

4. Read Matthew 19:13-14 again; then describe how children are treated in your congregation.

21

> *Now there was a Pharisee named Nicodemus, a leader of the Jews. He came to Jesus by night and said to him, "Rabbi, we know that you are a teacher who has come from God; for no one can do these signs that you do apart from the presence of God." Jesus answered him, "Very truly, I tell you, no one can see the kingdom of God without being born from above."*
>
> *(John 3:1-3)*

THE COMMUNITY FEELS SAFE AND ACCESSIBLE

Nicodemus may have come to Jesus by night because he wanted to meet him in a safe place, where his peers would not be present to sneer at or judge his questions or to make him suffer negative consequences for seeking Jesus. Jesus not only received him on his terms but also understood the deeper longing of his heart, which was to "see the kingdom of God." This is a perfect portrayal of the kind of community we need as we learn about God's kingdom and experience the presence of Christ.

Some of my more painful memories from childhood are of being laughed at, ridiculed, or put down by peers by whom I longed to be accepted. It is the rare child or youth who does not have similar experiences. Most people carry these kinds of memories into adulthood. They cause us to be skeptical of new opportunities for social gathering and acceptance. Part of our learning as we move toward adulthood is to develop coping mechanisms to deal with social disappointments such as these. In spite of previous hurts, it is possible for people of any age to enjoy healthy community, a place to be with others who have similar values, spend time together, tell stories, and have common experiences. Furthermore, to experience community that is fulfilling, we have to learn how to overcome these internal and external blocks that may be a part of our past or present situation. True Christian community is a place where this can happen regularly and consistently. Unfortunately, far too often our lack of sensitivity not only reduces the possibility of others experiencing true community, but it also brings about additional pain and rejection.

Anne, a young woman who had moved into a new community, attended one church for several Sundays and decided to visit the adult Bible study class. She was enthusiastically welcomed, since the class had not had any new members for some time. As the Bible study unfolded, however, she became uncomfortable. Several people made comments about "those people" who periodically came to the church to ask for food. Later, some people expressed disgust about the pressure in recent years to change the language referring to God, in order to satisfy the "feminists." When Anne explained that she had a friend who had been abused by her father and therefore had difficulty with God being referred to only as male, she sensed uncomfortable stares from some of the others. She decided not to return to the class—or to the church, for that matter. Frequently, we are unaware of how our comments or actions cause others to feel not welcome, unsafe, or even unwanted.

In describing hospitality, Henri Nouwen says:

Hospitality, therefore, means primarily the creation of a free space where the stranger can enter and become a friend instead of an enemy. Hospitality is not to change people, but to offer them space where change can take place. It is not to bring men and women over to our side, but to offer freedom not disturbed by dividing lines. It is not to lead our neighbor into a corner where there are no alternatives left, but to open a wide spectrum of options for choice and commitment. (From *Reaching Out: The Three Movements of the Spiritual Life*, by Henri J. M. Nouwen; page 51. © 1975 Henri J. M. Nouwen. Used by permission of Doubleday, a division of Random House, Inc.)

Just as Jesus often drew people into his presence and into relationship with him, with others around him, and with God, the second growing point is characterized by the feeling that *I want to belong here*. One senses a power and presence that goes deeper than words and discovers unconditional acceptance by other people and, in a deeper sense, by the very Spirit of God. A bond with others who also are experiencing that same accepting spirit begins to form. The bond runs deep and will outlast the many frailties and imperfections of human relationships.

In Paul's letter to the Ephesians, he offers many suggestions for personal and group interaction that portray Christ-like behavior:

> With all humility and gentleness, with patience, bearing with one another in love, making every effort to maintain the unity of the Spirit,...but speaking the truth in love, we must grow up in every way into him who is the head, into Christ... So then, putting away falsehood, let all of us speak the truth to our neighbors, for we are members of one another.... Put away from you all bitterness and wrath and anger and wrangling and slander...and be kind to one another, tenderhearted, forgiving one another, as God in Christ has forgiven you. Therefore be imitators of God, as beloved children, and live in love, as Christ loved us.
>
> (Ephesians 4:2-3, 15, 25, 31–5:2)

We must make every effort to influence any group we are part of to break down walls of judgment, prejudice, insensitivity, and rejection, in order to allow people to experience the ever-present Spirit of Christ.

CHRIST IS PRESENT WHEN WE GATHER IN HIS NAME

While experiencing the presence of Jesus Christ is transforming within an individual life, to experience Christ's Holy Spirit in community is what Pentecost is all about. Sadly, much of what happens within the life of the institutional church has little to do with knowing the real presence of Jesus Christ. Yet, it was the Holy Spirit that imparted power, joy, and energy to the early disciples.

> When the day of Pentecost had come, they were all together in one place. And suddenly from heaven there came a sound like the rush of a violent wind, and it filled the entire house where they were sitting. Divided tongues, as of fire, appeared among them, and a tongue rested on each of them. All of them were filled with the Holy Spirit and began to speak in other languages, as the Spirit gave them ability.... [The crowd was] amazed and perplexed, saying to one another, "What does this mean?"... But Peter...raised his voice and addressed them.
>
> (Acts 2:1-4, 12, 14)

Peter's reply to the crowd was the first sermon of the new church. He told of his understanding of the remarkable things that God had done through Jesus Christ, especially raising Jesus from the dead, "[making] him both Lord and Messiah, this Jesus whom you crucified" (Acts 2:36). What Peter really witnessed to was the reality of the promise made by Jesus when he said, "For where two or three are gathered in my name, I am there among them" (Matthew 18:20). The

Application Questions

1. Consider Paul's list of Christ-like qualities in Ephesians 4 and think of times you have been in a group that displayed these qualities. How did this group know how to act?

2. Think of comments you have heard or actions you have seen that caused people within a group to feel not welcome and to pull away, perhaps never to return.

3. Identify some things that you could say or do to counter the negative or destructive elements of group interaction that cause people to feel unsafe or unwanted.

disciples were now actually experiencing what Jesus had promised. Could it be that the reality expressed by Jesus in this promise is at the heart of what is being discovered in our day as the power of small-group ministry? At the end of the Great Commission, Matthew reports Jesus' words: "And remember, I am with you always, to the end of the age" (Matthew 28:20b). This, too, is a promise that Jesus fulfills every time people gather in his name to share their faith with one another. Christian community is community in which the Holy Spirit is present.

What the disciples experienced on Pentecost has significant implications for our understanding of Christian community. First, they were gathered in one place to celebrate an important aspect of their faith (the commemoration of Pentecost, a Jewish holy day). They wanted Jesus to be with them. They undoubtedly were telling stories, as they had done frequently since the ascension of Jesus.

Next, they experienced the Holy Spirit, present with them in a new and different way. They felt the power and encouragement of the Spirit, and they sensed the presence in a sound that was like the rush of a mighty wind in the room where they were gathered, and by tongues as of fire that rested over each of them. Also, they realized their differences as they spoke in different languages, but they were not hindered by those differences.

Finally, they were compelled to tell others what had happened and went out to tell their stories. Peter fearlessly spoke publicly about their firm belief in the risen Christ, who had now come to be present with them through the Holy Spirit. This was so exciting that he had to shout it to the world.

How often does this happen in our time? Have we become so oblivious to the presence of Christ that we hardly recognize what a remarkable happening it is? It is often the person new to the faith who catches the remarkable nature of Christ's presence and calls it to the attention of others.

Maria had long ago grown disenchanted with Sunday worship, feeling it did not address issues with which she struggled. At the invitation of a friend, she began participating in a weekly Bible study group. The time consisted of reading and studying passages of Scripture, discussing stories from each others' lives that related to the Scripture, and praying. The group would celebrate the Lord's Supper periodically. Maria has invited several other friends to attend the same group. When describing the group to her brother, she said, "I have come to experience the real presence of Christ. When we are together, I imagine Christ's presence is just as the disciples must have known him." It is the presence of Christ's Spirit that makes Christian community what it is.

How would it be if every person who enters the door of the church says silently, *Hello, Jesus. I am here.* And when you greet another person by saying his or her name out loud, you also say silently to yourself, *The Spirit of Christ is here.* In fact, we could even say that out loud to each other!

The apostle Paul's experience of the presence of Christ was so powerful that he identified the gathered community of Jesus' followers and other believers in the risen Christ as "one body in Christ" (Romans 12:5). He also said that Christ is "head over all things for the church, which is his body, the fullness of him who fills all in all" (Ephesians 1:22-23). The names *body of Christ* and *church* have stayed with us, but do we really experience the power and significance of the reality of Christ's presence from which they grew? The answer is both yes and no, but probably more of the latter.

Application Questions

1. When have you experienced Christ's presence in Christian community?

2. What made the experience of Christian community stand apart from other groups or gatherings?

3. What did others say or do that made the Spirit of Christ evident?

4. What keeps Christ from being present in some groups?

5. How can we be more receptive to Christ's presence and share this awareness with others?

24

As we think about moments in our lives when we have grown significantly in the faith, we often recall those who were around us at the time. Why? It is quite likely that they embodied one or more of the qualities of Christian community and that their behavior and words drew us in. Though we may not have had words for it, we were experiencing the Spirit of Christ in community.

LIFE STORIES ARE TOLD

As community develops and one is drawn in, bits and pieces of daily life are shared. They may be only fragments, a comment here and there out of experiences, thoughts, or feelings; but when the level of acceptance and interaction is comfortable, the snippets become stories that hold the heartbeat of life. A mother talks about her children; a worker tells of an incident on the job; senior members reminisce; old and new memories become precious. Whether a person actually speaks is not as important as feeling that the conversation and interaction of the group includes him or her and is about what he or she cares about.

A group of men who call themselves the Muffin Crew get together one Sunday a month in the church kitchen at five-thirty in the morning to bake thirty to forty dozen muffins for the morning fellowship time. The stories begin as soon as they gather, with each one telling about the latest adventures, struggles, and events in his life. Are these stories critical to the developing faith for each member? Generally not, if they are taken one by one; however, the feeling of acceptance, caring, and accountability among the members has a positive impact on their faith. The one who is struggling with the end of a relationship finds support as well as challenge, and perhaps a few new insights. The one celebrating a new accomplishment finds support, encouragement, and a reality check that keeps the rest of life in perspective. As they welcomed a new pastor on his first Sunday morning, they explained, "Here in the kitchen we are the church for one another."

Community that is really Christian community is a remarkable thing. In it we find that our own personal stories—our lives—are valued. We are willing to place them in the hands of others who can be supportive, who can challenge, and who can help us maintain perspective and balance. In Christian community our stories and our lives are drawn into the presence of one another and of Christ.

THE POWER OF PRAYER

On the Day of Pentecost, when the disciples received the Holy Spirit, Peter preached a powerful sermon that encouraged many of those in the streets of Jerusalem to believe in the risen Christ. The account in Acts 2 closes the story with these words: "So those who welcomed his message were baptized, and that day about three thousand persons were added. They devoted themselves to the apostles' teaching and fellowship, to the breaking of bread and the prayers" (Acts 2:41-42). Communal prayer is a vital aspect of Christian community. As we pray together, the ever-present Spirit of Christ unites us in bonds of peace and unity.

Many churches use intercessory prayer during worship as an effective means to lift up needs of members of the church body, the local community, and the world. For people new to the faith, this is a significant witness to the power of praying for others and is a way of showing faith and trust in God's healing touch.

Application Questions

1. What was the last group you were part of where you felt heard as you told about an incident from your life? What did it feel like?

2. What is the difference between participating in an experience at a workshop or conference with people you will never meet again and being part of an ongoing small group of friends in your own congregation?

3. How can we help small groups in the church learn to value one another's stories and life experiences in a nonthreatening, redemptive way?

4. How can we help others become aware of the ever-present Spirit of Christ?

Application Questions

1. List ways—besides the common form of using prayer as an opening devotion—that prayer can be used effectively in a group gathering.

2. How can people grow in confidence in offering communal prayers?

The Lord's Prayer is a communal prayer. The opening words ("Our Father") and the additional pronouns, which are in plural form, acknowledge the community nature for which Jesus intended the prayer to be used. It speaks to the importance of a communal experience of the presence of Christ, especially in the act of prayer. The Lord's Prayer helps to usher in an experience of God's realm within our midst. Other prayers that we pray in community can also have a similar impact.

CLOSING

The apostle Paul was aware of the importance and value of Christian community. In his letters, he immediately established a rapport with the recipients and invited them to be aware of the presence of the risen Christ. He began many of his letters with the words "Grace to you and peace from God our Father and the Lord Jesus Christ."

We would do well, whenever we gather in Christian community, to acknowledge Christ's presence through our words, demeanor, actions, and thoughts. As we work to improve the quality of Christian community wherever it manifests itself, we can help people to know Jesus Christ in a more significant way and grow as followers of Christ in all that they do. Jesus' final words to the disciples after giving the Great Commission were "And remember, I am with you always, to the end of the age" (Matthew 28:20b). Our biggest challenge is being convinced of this and living in a way that reflects our awareness of Christ's presence. What we, as spiritual leaders, must do is to proclaim the good news that Christ is with us and can be known by others through our actions and way of life.

Chapter Four

Growing Point Three:

I Experience God

Beginning relationship

Integrating God's Word with life experiences

Experiencing Christian community

O God, you are my God, I seek you,
    my soul thirsts for you;
my flesh faints for you,
    as in a dry and weary land
        where there is no water.
So I have looked upon you in the sanctuary,
    beholding your power and glory.
Because your steadfast love is better than life,
    my lips will praise you.
So I will bless you as long as I live;
    I will lift up my hands and call on your name.
                                    (Psalm 63:1-4)

The writer of Psalm 63 expresses the deep desires of the human soul: to know God and to be known by God. When one has a beginning relationship with the Spirit of Christ, one's own spirit takes the first small steps that lead out toward the flowing stream of God's grace and spirit. Experiencing the presence of the Spirit of Christ in community shows that there are hands and arms upon which to depend. New steps in faith emerge as one learns that this stream is part of a long and powerful story, God's story. The discovery begins to unfold that the one who knows each name and each story is God.

Jesus' conversation with the woman at the well in Samaria (John 4:7-26) was just one of many times that Jesus drew people from the world of their daily existence and experiences into the larger awareness of God's realm. When Jesus said, "The water that I will give will become in them a spring of water gushing up to eternal life" (John 4:14b), he was connecting the woman's daily personal experience with the Word of God.

The third growing point focuses on the integration of God's Word into our life experiences so that we may experience God. In this section, we will explore several ways in which this may happen.

ATTENTIVENESS TO GOD'S WORD: THE COMMUNITY GATHERS IN WORSHIP

In Psalm 42:1-2, we read, "As a deer longs for flowing streams, so my soul longs for you, O God. My soul thirsts for God, for the living God." As human beings, we long for a relationship with God because of God's love for us. In worship, the human longing to know God and God's continual reaching out to the human heart come together. People come to worship with an attitude of expectation and anticipation; they want something to happen that will help them experience God's presence.

A prospective pastor was visiting with a staff parish committee. At the introductory meeting, one of the members turned to the pastor and said, "I come to worship in order to meet God, but lately God does not seem to be there very often. Can you explain how you, as worship leader, can help the people who are present to experience God?"

This parishioner was expressing not only her hopes and expectations for new leadership that would help worship in her church to be vital, but she was also giving voice to the deep longing of the human soul to meet God. This longing is met by engaging with God's word through the Scriptures. It happens in personal Bible study and devotions, small-group Bible study, and in worship of the larger community. The gathering of the community in regular worship presents the opportunity for people to discover how their own stories are part of God's larger story.

A pastor was visiting an older parishioner who expressed her sadness that she could no longer go to church and worship with the congregation as she had for years. Then she said, "Even though I can't go, I still get dressed in my Sunday best and sit in this chair. I think of all the people who used to sit around me, and I find myself right there in church." Her experience was often enhanced by watching her church's service that was broadcast live on a local television station. When asked what the most important part of this experience is, she said, "It is hearing God's Word and knowing that I am part of it."

Being in church is about being present with the gathered community in the presence of God. One weekend I was with my family in a strange city far from home. Wanting very much to attend a service of worship on Sunday morning, we made our way to the nearest church. We entered a large beautiful sanctuary, were greeted in a friendly way by the ushers, and offered seats. We looked around at others seated near us, who were all strangers at this point. The prelude began, followed by the opening hymn and processional. Within moments, we found

Make me to know your ways, O LORD; teach me your paths. Lead me in your truth, and teach me, for you are the God of my salvation; for you I wait all day long.

(Psalm 25:4-5)

ourselves immersed in a service of Christian worship that was comforting and reassuring. We did not sense that we were among strangers; rather, we were in the gathered community of those seeking to learn and follow God's way.

In vital worship, attention is given to the reading, hearing, and interpretation of God's Word in such a way that each person is drawn into the biblical story and experiences the story coming to life in today's world. Worship leaders, particularly the preacher who interprets the Word, must be aware that corporate worship provides a crucial place and time where people can interact with God and explore their own stories in the context of God's larger story.

God Speaks Through Scripture: My Story Fits in God's Story

When families living in rural America hear the parable of the sower and the soils, they are drawn into the story. Farmers planting their fields sense that when Jesus of Nazareth described the seed that fell in rocky places or the thorns that overgrew the seeds (Matthew 13:3-9), he clearly understood their world and the challenges of daily life.

Likewise, the landowner finds in the Scripture stories about tenants who take advantage of their boss's absence (Matthew 21:33-41); those about to be married find stories about wedding banquets (Matthew 22:1-14); and those who are bruised in body or spirit find stories of healing and restoration of life. People long to hear that the Scriptures are about them.

"Your word is a lamp to my feet and a light to my path," we affirm with the writer of Psalm 119:105. Why does the Bible hold such power and ability to convey the voice of God? Second Timothy responds with another affirmation: "All scripture is inspired by God and is useful for teaching, for reproof, for correction, and for training in righteousness" (2 Timothy 3:16). To speak of the biblical text as being inspired is generally taken to mean that there is a divine nature and authority inherent in the writings.

Jesus stood up in the synagogue in Nazareth and read from the Scriptures: "'The Spirit of the Lord is upon me, because he has anointed me to bring good news to the poor'... Then he began to say to them, 'Today this scripture has been fulfilled in your hearing'" (Luke 4:16-21). The writers of the Gospels often show how Jesus' life and ministry fit into the ongoing stories of the Hebrew Scriptures and fulfilled elements of older stories and prophecies. Their intention was to help the reader not only to hear and know the stories but also to believe in Jesus Christ and, furthermore, to find new life through him. As we read in John 20:30: "Now Jesus did many other signs in the presence of his disciples, which are not written in this book. But these are written so that you may come to believe that Jesus is the Messiah, the Son of God, and that through believing you may have life in his name."

The discovery that our personal stories belong in God's larger story is part of the dawning of deeper belief in Jesus Christ as God's Son, and the beginning of new life in him. The older woman who said that she gets dressed for church and sits in her favorite chair also said, "Then I get out my Bible and read the Scriptures, and I think of all the things I can remember about how I fit into those stories." This woman has found one of the valuable parts of a developing faith: to read or hear God's Word and to let one's own story be found within God's larger story.

Application Questions

1. Make a list of the elements in your worship services that encourage participants to be attentive to God's Spirit.

2. What preparations are necessary on the part of worship leaders so that the Spirit of God can be experienced more fully by those who gather?

Application Questions

1. What elements of worship help participants hear God's story in such a way that it has personal meaning for them?

2. How are people encouraged in worship to reflect on their own stories in the context of God's larger story?

3. What steps could be taken in your congregation to encourage encountering God's larger story?

29

Meaning-Making: Relating Faith to Life

When Jesus stood up in the synagogue in Nazareth and read from the Hebrew Scriptures, he was connecting the purpose and meaning of his life to the long-term historic emphasis of Jewish prophecy and covenant with God. The process of meaning-making is that of sorting out the bits and pieces of daily life in the context of a larger purpose or understanding.

Week after week in a divorce support group, Katherine would tell about her grief, anger, and frustration. She would often end in tears, but also with the phrase "I keep saying to God, 'There must be a better plan for my life, because this one is getting ridiculous.'" Gradually, Katherine was able to sort out the pieces, one by one, and gain a new perspective on life. As she did this, she insisted that what helped with her healing was her faith that she could count on God's constancy and love, which was reaffirmed for her during worship every Sunday.

When one becomes part of a faith community—through worship, prayer, study, small-group ministries, and other meaningful experiences—one's own story begins to blend with the larger story and purpose of the community. The formative aspect of Scripture has the most effect when we allow it to penetrate our lives and speak to us, both individually and in community. As concerted efforts are made to help people connect their stories with God's story, they can more successfully make meaning out of the various events of daily life. This is clearly seen when people go through the death of a loved one and find—in the words of comfort, Scriptures, and prayers—those powerful elements of faith, hope, and assurance that give them strength to carry on.

Among the powerful images of healing and restoration following the tragedy of the school shootings in recent years were the funeral services held for the victims. Classmates, teachers, and community leaders surrounded the family members with deep expressions of faith and love, in order to help put the pieces of life back together. These same dynamics are vital for individuals who appear in nearly every congregation on a weekly basis carrying in their hearts often-unspoken stories of sorrow and sadness, frustration and failure, or even of joy and celebration. Why can't we apply the tools of our faith, the words of Scripture, and the resources of worship to all events of life on a more consistent basis?

When a community is safe and secure, so that people are able to reflect on their own experiences, and when others reflect with them and hold them accountable for decisions made, routes to newer meaning are created that can be trusted and followed. These routes lead to meaning that is consistent with the values and teachings we learn from Jesus Christ about relationships with others and about God's creative, redeeming love.

Experiencing God Through the Sacrament of Baptism

In baptism, a person is claimed by the faith community as a child of God and a member of the body of Christ. Although in all baptisms we recognize that we are dependent upon God, this is powerfully symbolized in infant baptism. It is clear to us that there is nothing an infant has to do or can do to earn God's grace. It is a free, unmerited gift from God. Of course, the same is true no matter what our stage in life.

Application Questions

1. What are some indications that people in your faith community are able to draw on their faith to make meaning in their lives?

2. What would be different if more emphasis in your worship or community life were placed on helping participants make meaning of life's events?

30

Baptism is sometimes referred to as the sacrament of belonging. Through baptism, we recognize that "God knows my name" and that "My life story is part of God's story. I belong to God!"

Individuals are baptized; however, baptism is not an individual event. One is baptized into a community. Each time a person is baptized, everyone in the community remembers that they, too, are a child of God. And although we are baptized only once, our entire faith journey might be described as living into our baptism.

It is not uncommon to find parents who want their child baptized, even though they may be on the fringe of a faith community and have not attended worship for years. They may be responding to an inner recognition that each person is a child of God; therefore, they want their new child to be known and named by God. They may also be responding to their own longing for a closer relationship with God. The preparation for baptism, the baptism itself, and the continuing support of the congregation can become opportunities for beginning relationships with the new parents.

For many parents who are active in the life of a congregation, the experience of a child's baptism is a high moment in their own faith journeys and leads to continued growth in the faith.

Regardless of the person's age, the sacrament of baptism and all that surrounds it is an important moment for the person being baptized, for family members, and for the congregation. It is a significant way in which we experience God.

Experiencing God Through the Sacrament of Holy Communion

The apostle Paul underscores the communal nature of Holy Communion: "Because there is one bread, we who are many are one body, for we all partake of the one bread" (1 Corinthians 10:17). Through the words of the ritual, the responses of the people, and the elements of bread and wine, Communion not only symbolizes the presence of Jesus Christ and the sacrifice he made on the cross, but it also recalls and reestablishes the community experienced by the disciples at the Last Supper. In the ritual and through the physical act of receiving the elements, participants are made more aware of the real presence of Jesus Christ. He enters not only into the gathered community but also into every heart and soul that is receptive. For the person poised to take new steps in faith, participating in Communion in a meaningful way is a concrete experience that helps form meaning and memory, draws one's own story into the heart of God's story, and opens the door for the discovery of gifts and being called forth to serve.

The service of Communion allows us to find ourselves seated at the banquet table set for us by Jesus Christ. With these gentle words, Rueben Job explains the powerful effect that coming to the Lord's Table has in forming community:

There is one place where everyone is absolutely equal, a place where all class, social, racial, economic, educational and every other distinction evaporates as a morning mist under a bright summer sun. That place of absolute equality is at the Lord's Table. Here, as at no other place, we realize our oneness with Christ and our oneness with each other. Each person stands on equal ground; none is higher or lower. We all come incomplete and broken, we all come seeking wholeness and

Application Questions

1. Identify the ways in which people who are being baptized in your congregation are aware of being named and claimed by God.

2. What steps are taken by people who are responsible for meeting with parents prior to the baptism of children? How are the parents encouraged to think carefully about their own faith and relationship with Christ?

Application Questions

1. In the celebration of Holy Communion in your church, what contributes to an awareness on the part of the participants of being at the table set and served by Jesus Christ?

2. How are participants in Holy Communion helped to feel drawn into God's larger story of acceptance, forgiveness, and redemption?

healing. We all come needy and with empty hands. And soon or late we all realize that only God can mend us, heal us, redeem us, and feed us on the bread of life. (From *A Wesleyan Spiritual Reader,* by Rueben P. Job; page 60. © 1998 Abingdon Press. Used by permission.)

Holy Communion is a remarkable sign of the reign of God. It is a banquet of the Kingdom, where all people are brought to the Lord's Table and are served by Christ himself. In Communion, we come to the source of the living water. When we come fractured and bruised by the experiences of life, we can find healing, redemption, and focus for life. When we come in a spirit of celebration of the joys and happiness of life, we experience affirmation and mutual celebration with the Spirit of Christ.

Growing Point Four:

I Am Called

Beginning relationship

Identifying gifts
and responding
to God's call

Integrating God's Word
with life experiences

Experiencing Christian
community

As he walked along, he saw a man blind from birth. His disciples asked him, "Rabbi, who sinned, this man or his parents, that he was born blind?" Jesus answered, "Neither this man nor his parents sinned; he was born blind so that God's works might be revealed in him."... When he had said this, he spat on the ground and made mud with the saliva and spread the mud on the man's eyes, saying to him, "Go, wash in the pool of Siloam" (which means Sent). Then he went and washed and came back able to see. The neighbors and those who had seen him before as a beggar began to ask, "Is this not the man who used to sit and beg?" Some were saying, "It is he." Others were saying, "No, but it is someone like him." He kept saying, "I am the man." But they kept asking him, "Then how were your eyes opened?" He answered, "The man called Jesus made mud, spread it on my eyes, and said to me, 'Go to Siloam and wash.' Then I went and washed and received my sight." (John 9:1-11)

Jesus met a man who was born blind. He had eyes, but he had never been able to see. The disciples were concerned with why he was blind—was it because of the sin of his parents or something that he had done wrong? Jesus recognized that through this man others could come to experience the work of God. So Jesus bent down and made some mud, put it on the man's eyes, and instructed him to go to a pool and wash his eyes. The man did so and came back seeing and glorifying God.

This story can be considered a depiction of how unique, personal gifts and talents can be uncovered and used to glorify God. Within each of us there are gifts and resources that often go unused for the building up of God's people.

The fourth growing point addresses the matter of more consistently discovering giftedness and call within the people of faith. As we explore discipleship, we must look at ways people identify their gifts and talents and are called to use those gifts for the building up of the community of faith. Let us return to the story of Jesus with the man born blind and see how it comes about.

First, the Man Was Found by Jesus

When we are found by Christ, the Holy Spirit awakens a new awareness within us that we are recognized and named, that we have gifts and talents that are valued, and that we are called (challenged) to use our gifts in service to God and others. This may happen as we receive the gentle touch of Christ's love, open our lives to the Spirit of Christ as revealed in community, and find ourselves immersed in God's larger story of redemption and love made known through Jesus Christ.

On the other hand, we may encounter Jesus Christ through another person, through a life-shaking event, or through Scriptures. In whatever way it happens, Jesus finds us and call us to use the gifts that God has given us.

Next, Jesus Ignores All the Excuses and Opens the Man's Eyes

Notice that in the case of the man who was born blind, other people found various reasons why he should stay blind—it was just the way his life was meant to be. Jesus ignored them and pointed out that the man's blindness was going to become a way for God's work to be done through him. Notice also that Jesus did not ask the man if he wanted to see; Jesus just opened his eyes so that he could see. That is often the way it works. While we are getting accustomed to new discoveries about God and Jesus Christ, we may be staying timidly on the sidelines, not wanting to be noticed. But Jesus sees something in us and calls it forth. He challenges us to move out into deeper water and to trust the flow of the current to hold us up as we learn to float or swim.

Now, a word of caution: At times, because of overly zealous recruiters, people who are just discovering new gifts and abilities feel as if they are being pounced upon, so they withdraw in fright before they ever get a chance to develop their gifts. Like the man healed of his blindness, people who are discovering their gifts and talents must be able to grow in their faith. This amplifies the need to pay attention to the aspects identified in the discussion of other growing points, such as providing a welcoming, compassionate, and respectful presence and applying those insights to help people uncover unidentified gifts and call—at their own pace, not because we desperately need a person to teach the third grade Sunday school class.

Finally, the Man Confirms His Newfound Faith in Jesus

The fourth growing point relates to discovering our gifts and talents and allowing Jesus Christ to work wonders in our lives. It is about going to the pool called Sent, washing off the mud and the scales, coming back to glorify God, and letting God use our talents. It is about having our eyes opened when they have been sealed. It is about being called out by the Spirit of God to do things that we never dreamed we could do, because Jesus is there opening our eyes and helping us to discover new talents and new abilities that we never knew we had. It is

Jesus heard that they had driven [the man who had been born blind] out, and when he found him, he said, "Do you believe in the Son of Man?" He answered, "And who is he, sir? Tell me, so that I may believe in him." Jesus said to him, "You have seen him, and the one speaking with you is he." He said, "Lord, I believe." And he worshiped him.

(John 9:35-38)

34

about the beginning of the process of allowing our lives to be transformed by the Spirit of Christ, a process that continues through our lifetime as we grow in faithful discipleship.

Discovery of Gifts and Talents

Gifts refer to the gifts of the Spirit, as listed in 1 Corinthians 12:4-11 and Ephesians 4:11-13. Spiritual gifts are not given to ensure the survival of the institutional church; rather, they are gifts given by God so that the world might be transformed. The faithful use of spiritual gifts enables people to be the church, the body of Christ.

Talents are often used to describe the broad scope of God-given personal qualities, abilities, and skills. As talents are honed by the experiences of life and infused by the power and presence of the Spirit of Christ, we become grace-filled people with an ability to serve and minister to others in all aspects of our lives. Great satisfaction and reward can be found in discovering talents that can be used for the benefit of God's world and people. The more talents are used to the glory of God, the more they unfold and give birth to new possibilities.

The discovery of spiritual gifts and talents is a process by which people not only identify their unique gifts and talents but also become moved by God's spirit of usefulness and respond out of a desire to be useful to someone or something within God's creation. The issue is what we do within the Christian community to encourage each person to discover his or her gifts and talents. How can we more effectively help people discover their spiritual gifts and talents, develop them, and put them to good use? We must continue to ask these questions and look for answers within the context of our faith communities as we help people grow into discipleship.

When floods hit northwest Minnesota and North Dakota in the spring of 1997, more than five hundred work teams from all over the country responded during the ensuing two years to provide more than half a million hours of volunteer labor to help families clean up, rebuild, and repair their lives. Many of the people in those work teams did not think they were skilled in carpentry, flood cleanup, or the many tasks of disaster recovery. Still, they contributed an immeasurable amount of help to individuals, families, and communities. Some of the volunteers had skills and expertise learned over a lifetime; some gained new skills as they worked; and some gave primarily their time and expressions of care and concern. Together, the volunteer work teams made a big difference in helping the more than 100,000 people who were seriously affected by the floods put their lives back together. People returned home having experienced the presence of Christ as they used their gifts and talents to benefit others.

Gifts of the Spirit and our particular talents and abilities are all God-given characteristics that define who we are as individuals and as community. They are part of the wonder of God's creation. In our baptism, we offered ourselves to be conscious partners with God in living and growing as children of God. Responding to this call is an ongoing process of living out our baptism as followers and disciples of Christ.

We sometimes ask people in our churches to do particular jobs because we believe they have the skills and abilities to do the tasks, but we fail to consider if they are aware of the Holy Spirit at work within their lives. Sometimes these people do well with the given tasks, but they have difficulty seeing that Christ is at work through them and the work they are doing. They may be doing the job

Now there are varieties of gifts, but the same Spirit; and there are varieties of services, but the same Lord; and there are varieties of activities, but it is the same God who activates all of them in everyone. To each is given the manifestation of the Spirit for the common good.

(1 Corinthians 12:4-7)

The gifts he gave were that some would be apostles, some prophets, some evangelists, some pastors and teachers, to equip the saints for the work of ministry, for building up the body of Christ, until all of us come to the unity of the faith and of the knowledge of the Son of God, to maturity, to the measure of the full stature of Christ.

(Ephesians 4:11-13)

Application Questions

1. List at least five people you know who use their gifts, talents, and resources to meet the needs around them. Identify the gifts or talents they use and the needs that they address.

2. Identify times in the past year when you felt God's call to use a personal skill or talent to meet a need.

3. Describe to someone in the group a spiritual gift you believe you have. Talk together about needs to which that gift could respond.

4. If you were to meet Jesus Christ today, what gifts or talents might he recognize in you?

5. Think of the congregation with whom you worship. Make a quick list of qualities, talents, or gifts they have that are not being called upon. How might you (or your ministry team) help people recognize these gifts and call them forth?

out of a sense of obligation, sometimes even guilt. Discouragement and lack of joy are commonplace among people who serve with little sense of having been called and empowered by God.

RECOGNIZING NEEDS TO WHICH ONE'S GIFTS AND TALENTS RESPOND

Every student of chemistry learns early that when certain chemicals are brought together under the right conditions, a chemical reaction will follow. Sometimes it is immediate like an explosion; sometimes it occurs more slowly, taking minutes, hours, or days. At times the reaction produces heat or light; at other times it requires one or both in order to happen.

Within the realm of our faith, there are also powerful reactions that occur as certain elements come together under the right conditions. When the awakening of one's personal gifts and talents blends with the perception of specific needs to which one can respond—all within an environment where the Spirit of Christ can be experienced—new things begin to happen. As spiritual leaders, we can pay closer attention to what it takes for the right elements to interact so that new things happen as people recognize needs to which they are called to respond.

Some elements that often enhance the process include:
- hearing stories of others who have used their gifts in creative, helpful ways;
- experiencing the call or tug of Christ's Spirit;
- feeling affirmed and appreciated for what one has to offer;
- not being forced to respond beyond one's understanding of what God is calling one to do;
- being willing to reach out and share;
- being supported and respected by the community;
- serving as part of a team or group;
- finding some aspects of enjoyment and fun as the task is carried out;
- having opportunities to learn new ways of doing things and gaining new skills;
- gaining clarity about the difference between God-given talents and Holy-Spirit-empowered spiritual gifts.

One of the greatest challenges in our churches today is to not waste the gifts and talents available. A process of gifts discernment can help the faith community to identify the gifts and talents present. A variety of tools and resources are available to assist in this process. For more information on recommended resources, contact: Office of Stewardship Ministries, General Board of Discipleship, P.O. Box 340003, Nashville, TN 37203-0003. Phone: 877-899-2780.

Frequently, in developing ideas for specific mission or service projects, or in developing plans to meet certain needs within the church or community, various needs may surface to which people feel called to respond. It is good when that happens, but the matter of recognizing needs to which one can respond with one's gifts and talents is much broader and deeper than just carrying out specific ministry projects. It goes far beyond surveys of gifts and talents with lists of possible service opportunities. It has to do with an entire lifestyle of faithfulness and discipleship.

The recognition of the needs to which our gifts and talents may respond has much to do with the presence of Christ and our readiness to be open to the moving of the Holy Spirit in our lives.

Being Called Into Service and Ministry

As we discover our spiritual gifts and talents and feel the tug on our hearts to use them in fruitful ways for the betterment of God's creation, we are actually responding to the call we received at our baptism. It is a call from God to live out our lives in service and ministry as disciples of Christ. *The Book of Discipline of The United Methodist Church* makes this clear: "All Christians are called to minister wherever Christ would have them serve and witness in deeds and words that heal and free. This ministry of all Christians in Christ's name and spirit is both a gift and a task. The gift is God's unmerited grace; the task is unstinting service." (From *The Book of Discipline of The United Methodist Church—1996;* ¶¶ 105–6. Copyright © 1996 by The United Methodist Publishing House. Used by permission.)

An appropriate and important role of the church community is to help people recognize and name their gifts and find ways in which they may be used. A critical step in this process is to work continually at identifying, clarifying, and selecting the various ways the church can use its gifts and resources for the transformation of the world. In other words, the Body as a whole must be receptive to the presence of Jesus Christ as he chooses to identify blind spots and open eyes that have been closed. This occurs through

- small groups that study the Scriptures, pray, and ask God to help open eyes to the needs around them and help them find new avenues for ministry;
- preaching and worship that encourages individuals to open up to the neighborhood and community with the sensitivity and compassion of Jesus;
- a clear vision of what it means to be the body of Christ at work in the community, and living toward that vision;
- sensitivity to those who live in poverty or who find themselves on the margins of society, especially children and youth;
- a shared ministry process that helps people identify their gifts, find ways to use them, and be supported in service.

Sometimes the call surprises us: "You want me to teach Sunday school? I don't know anything about the Bible, let alone know how to teach!" "You want me to spend all night in a homeless shelter? Are you kidding?"

Often, we shrug off those little nudges that come from within or from others in the faith community. We think of all the things others would say about why we should not do this or that, and we hide—especially from Jesus—hoping that no one will notice us. Far too frequently we make sure we are far enough away that we believe even Jesus will not find us.

A youth group became caught up in the rush of activity following a devastating series of tornadoes in southern Minnesota in the spring of 1998. They decided to give up a weekend retreat to help clean debris from fields so that the farmers could plant their crops. Some of the youth went reluctantly, grumbling most of the way to the fields. After meeting the farm family and joining up with volunteers from the local community, the group joined in prayer and headed to the fields. At the end of several long days of hard work, the youth returned to their homes and reported to their congregation the next Sunday: "It was a fantastic experience! Nothing in the world is more wonderful than finding out you have skills and talents that meet someone else's need."

Application Questions

1. Identify the people within your congregation who have discovered a sense of call. What are some of the specific gifts they have discovered and used in response to their call?

2. List the jobs that people are asked to fulfill that do not have the feeling of call but are more accurately thought of as filling leadership positions. What can be done to decrease the number of jobs so that people serve out of a sense of shared ministry.

3. How can people be helped to see the work they do in their everyday lives as an opportunity to live out their Christian discipleship?

The greatest challenge for most congregations is to explore and find new ways to identify needs in the community and in areas of mission or service and then to place those needs before the people in ways that match the spiritual gifts, talents, knowledge, skills, and resources with needs.

One congregation has added a "mission moment" to nearly every service of worship, just prior to the closing hymn. Someone tells about an aspect of mission or service, encouraging others to give prayer support and to lend a hand if it seems appropriate. The leaders of worship and of the mission ministry team have been challenged to find new ways of helping connect the gifts of members of the congregation with the needs felt or expressed.

Summary

Let us return to the encounter of Jesus with the man who was born blind. The process of meeting Jesus Christ, having him touch our blind eyes, and sending us to the pool called Sent to wash away the mud and crust of the world so our eyes will be opened is participation in the miracle of healing and new life. As our gifts are identified, we are called and challenged to use our gifts. We are sent to meet needs as God cares for God's children and for the world. It is so dramatic that it transforms our lives and our outlook on the world. We begin to feel—at first silently within our hearts and then openly and honestly to others around us—that we can say with Paul: "It is no longer I who live, but it is Christ who lives in me" (Galatians 2:20).

Chapter Six

Growing Point Five:

I Walk With Others

Beginning relationship

Identifying gifts and
responding to God's call

Integrating God's Word
with life experiences

Experiencing Christian
community

Supporting one
another as we serve

This is my commandment, that you love one another as I have loved you. No one has greater love than this, to lay down one's life for one's friends. You are my friends if you do what I command you. I do not call you servants any longer, because the servant does not know what the master is doing; but I have called you friends, because I have made known to you everything that I have heard from my Father. You did not choose me but I chose you. And I appointed you to go and bear fruit, fruit that will last, so that the Father will give you whatever you ask him in my name. I am giving you these commands so that you may love one another.   (John 15:12-17)

A s Jesus lived and traveled from day to day with the twelve disciples, he modeled the important aspects of life in community. He showed that as one develops patterns and practices of a life of faith, being part of a supportive community provides consistency as each person continually learns to respond to the challenges of each stage in life. The disciples were with Jesus most of the time and, according to the accounts in the Gospels, were in frequent conversation with him, often about his teachings. At times they actively participated in his work. They helped serve the meal to the five thousand and were sent by Jesus to the villages with the news that "the kingdom of God has come near" (Luke 10:11b).

At other times, the disciples and Jesus were just together. On one occasion, they were in a boat on the Sea of Galilee. Jesus was asleep in the hold of the boat when a storm came up, catching them all off guard. Sometimes they walked along the roads and byways of Galilee. We can assume that they also spent many evenings together around a fire or dinner table. Though Jesus did not speak directly to the importance of supportive community, he demonstrated it as he began his ministry by choosing people to work and travel with him, people who would continue to be a community even in his absence. He also talked about the way he cared for the disciples and the way they would care for one another.

Jesus often found occasions to challenge the disciples to use their gifts in new ways that were appropriate to their development and position in life. After much teaching and healing on Jesus' part, and when Jesus felt that the disciples were ready, he "gave them power and authority over all demons and to cure diseases, and he sent them out to proclaim the kingdom of God and to heal" (Luke 9:1-2). When he felt that Peter, John, and James were ready, he took them to the mountain to pray, and Jesus was transfigured before them (Luke 9:28-36). Even after Jesus was no longer physically present, the disciples continued to gather as a supportive community (Acts 1:13-14), to worship, pray, and wait until Jesus' return. In fact, throughout the stories of the early church recorded in Acts and the Epistles, the disciples and other church leaders gathered regularly as the church.

Within the church, some people have become immune to the inner longing for such community and support. Nevertheless, the need for it does not disappear. The fifth growing point focuses on a significant area for growth in the faith as it encourages involvement in ongoing, supportive community to help us relate our gifts to true missional needs to which we can respond. The following elements contribute to this growing point:
- opportunities to serve and our ability to respond;
- challenges appropriate to stages in life;
- participation in a supportive community;
- experiences of the joy of service and discipleship leading to transformation of life.

OPPORTUNITIES TO SERVE AND OUR ABILITY TO RESPOND

Jesus' life was a continual unfolding of opportunities to be of service. In fact, it was often difficult to get beyond the constant presence of people needing attention, healing, and insights for living. Jesus' eyes of caring and compassion were always aware of the needs of others. The disciples saw the same situations and people that Jesus did; but rather than recognize them as opportunities for service, they often saw them as obstacles that blocked the experiences they wanted for themselves.

When the children crowded around, the disciples tried to push them away; but Jesus invited the children to sit on his lap as he taught about God's kingdom. When the crowds of people were tired and hungry, the disciples wanted to send them off to get something to eat. Jesus insisted that they should stay, because he saw this as an opportunity to feed them, both physically and spiritually.

Just as in Jesus' time, the list of needs and opportunities to serve is endless. Often, we become insensitive to the ways we can serve, just as a person's hearing loses sensitivity as one learns to tune out unwanted noises. The ability to perceive needs and opportunities is influenced by one's point of view and the condition of one's spiritual heart. Participating in supportive community has a positive influence on the discovery and use of gifts and talents. As one's heart and spirit are open to a realized presence of Christ, one's eyes begin to open to needs and opportunities to serve as Jesus would have served. Also, the more one responds to needs, the more other opportunities begin to unfold and manifest themselves.

Ron is the father of a youth who was preparing to go on a mission trip with his church group. The pastor of the church turned to Ron to ask if he would be willing to go along as an adult counselor. Ron had never done anything like that before and felt reluctant because he feared being asked to give leadership in issues relating to faith. But when he was assured by the pastor that he would not be put on the spot, Ron agreed to go along. As he had fearfully anticipated, the group got into several deep discussions about why they were serving in the name of Christ. Nonetheless, Ron entered into the conversations and offered his opinions. Later, he had some long talks with the pastor about his faith and prayed for new insights and wisdom.

To everyone's surprise, when the youth returned home and planned their report to the congregation the next Sunday morning, Ron asked if he could say a few words. His report turned into a witness of how he had grown in faith and now wanted to help with the Habitat for Humanity project in their community. Ron's involvement with mission projects grew from those initial steps to leading a Volunteers in Mission trip the next year.

This story points to the need for opportunities to serve and respond as needs and challenges continue to unfold. Since it is Christ who opens one's eyes to the gifts one has and to the needs in the world, it is also Christ who can help in making choices about how to respond.

CHALLENGES APPROPRIATE TO STAGES IN LIFE

A powerful impression that comes from the reported episodes in which Jesus recruits and invites his disciples to follow him is the complete readiness on their part to drop everything and follow him. We generally assume two things: (1) Jesus' presence and invitation were so compelling that it was impossible to refuse, and (2) the lives of the disciples were much simpler and more flexible than ours are today, thus allowing them to leave everything and follow Jesus.

The first assumption has to do with our experience of the presence of Christ. It is true that the presence of Jesus in person must have been compelling. His invitation to serve was heard and felt personally and persuasively. If the soon-to-be disciples had any doubts about who Jesus was, there was no ambiguity about what he was asking them to do and about what it would take to follow him. When Jesus was talking with Simon Peter about Simon's reluctance to leave his fishing boat, Jesus said, "Do not be afraid; from now on you will be catching people" (Luke 5:10).

Our situation is different from that of the disciples in one vital respect: Jesus is not physically present to offer the challenge in clear, undeniable terms. We need to offer settings in which people can experience the presence of the Spirit of Christ in recognizable ways. A high point of most annual conferences is the ordination service. The Minnesota Annual Conference has in recent years added a new feature to this service. At the end of the service, the bishop makes an invitation for people who feel a stirring of the heart to explore new avenues of service and ministry to come to the front where they can visit with members of

As Jesus was walking along, he saw a man called Matthew sitting at the tax booth; and he said to him, "Follow me." And he got up and followed him.

(Matthew 9:9)

For as in one body we have many members, and not all the members have the same function, so we, who are many, are one body in Christ, and individually we are members one of another. We have gifts that differ according to the grace given to us: prophecy, in proportion to faith; ministry, in ministering; the teacher, in teaching; the exhorter, in exhortation; the giver, in generosity; the leader, in diligence; the compassionate, in cheerfulness.

(Romans 12:4-8)

the board of ordained ministry and receive their prayers of support and encouragement. Nearly every year, ten or more people come forward to reflect on the movement of the Spirit within their lives.

Some congregations offer such an opportunity at the end of each service of worship, making sure that the setting is in keeping with the concerns expressed in the first growing point, beginning relationship. Such an invitation is not the typical altar call, for the emphasis is on the prayer and support related to discovery and use of gifts. It must be done with great care and respect for each individual's uniqueness and personal needs.

The "call to discipleship" or "prayer of dedication and service," which some pastors place following a sermon, has some of the same qualities: to serve as a time when people are encouraged to think of their own response to the message of the day. DISCIPLE Bible study classes have numerous opportunities to allow the participants to experience the compelling call from the Spirit of Christ to serve in new ways. It is not uncommon in such classes for people to acknowledge the desire to respond to a call to ministry that may have been heard and ignored earlier in life.

After worship one Sunday when the focus of the service had been on the mission statement of the congregation, Judy said to the pastor, "I am feeling something within me to which I need to respond. May I come and talk to you sometime?" Later that week in the pastor's office, Judy said, "I have developed some gifts and skills in my work that this congregation needs as we focus more clearly on our mission. I can't keep silent any longer, especially after Sunday's service. Tell me how I can fit in." Spiritual leaders today must be ready to help people respond appropriately to the voice of the Spirit working from within the heart to challenge and call forth one's gifts.

The second assumption, that the disciples' lives were much simpler and easier to change than ours, is seriously flawed. It may be that we have many things that tie us to a particular location. We can point to our varied responsibilities and commitments that keep us from being free. But how much of this is an excuse or delusion? Aren't we being rather arrogant to assume that we have more responsibilities than did the disciples? They, too, would have been expected to provide a livelihood for their spouses and children. In fact, their culture indicates the possible presence of grandparents or other relatives living in the same house for whom they may have had responsibility. We must take a new look at the powerful influence that the presence of Jesus Christ had upon those who truly allowed themselves to be open to the power and presence of the Spirit of God at work in and through him. We must allow ourselves and those around us to be open to the influence and impact of the realized presence of Jesus Christ.

As spiritual leaders, we sometimes are overly protective of our flock. Time and time again, a member of a committee on nominations and personnel will answer for someone the committee is considering for a new area of service, saying, "Oh, she wouldn't do that. She is so busy with her family." Instead, once the committee has prayerfully considered calling someone to an area of service that may seem out of the question, the Spirit of Christ should be given a chance to work wonders within the life of that person and let him or her decide whether to respond to the call.

More than once after preaching a sermon about taking the risk to respond to the leading of Christ's Spirit within our lives, I have been surprised later to find that a member of the church has heeded the call and is making plans to leave home, job, and perhaps the community to go out in a new direction. Such risk-taking points even more strongly to the invaluable role that supportive community must play in helping people discern appropriately that the call being heard is the right call to respond to at this point in life.

Betty had been a homemaker for twenty-six years, and her three children were grown and living away from home. She had filled many leadership roles within her church over the years. As her DISCIPLE Bible study group was discussing gifts and call to service, she told the group that something was stirring within her heart. She wanted to explore the volunteer coordinator position at a large church nearby, but she was concerned about her own lack of skill and what her church friends would say. The group gave Betty strong support, offered suggestions about how she could receive training, and assured her that they would not forget about her. With that encouragement, she applied for the position and entered into a new chapter of her life as a spiritual leader in a new church family. Some changes are more painful as we adjust to shifts in the world around us.

Following a church conference in a small Midwestern town, Bob, a long-time member of the church, told the others around the table that he was facing a difficult decision. The turkey farm that had been in his family for three generations was so successful that it had drawn the attention of the conglomerate that had bought all the other family turkey operations in the area. His was the only farm that continued to make a profit while not using food additives and questionable practices that challenged the environment. But his sources of food supply and access to the market were being squeezed shut by the conglomerate. Representatives of the conglomerate had visited him that day and had offered him a deal that would allow him to stay in operation if he would cooperate with their directives. His only other choice seemed to be to experience further difficulties and ultimately to close his operation, putting his sixteen employees out of work and leaving his own family without an income.

As he told details of the story, all of which were already too familiar to his friends, they gathered around and listened quietly. They offered a few suggestions and their support. Then one of them said, "We need to have a time of prayer as we ask God to guide Bob through this." The group joined hands and took turns praying for direction. Bob left knowing that Christ would go with him, and he could count on support from his friends in Christ, no matter how things turned out.

A month later, when a friend in Christ checked with him to see how it was going, Bob said that the inevitable had happened: He was closing down. However, he was using all the assets he could muster to provide counseling, training, and job relocation for the employees who were losing their jobs. He said he trusted that God would guide him into the future and would help him find new ways to use his own gifts. He even wondered out loud whether this might be the right time to heed the call that had been tugging at his heart for several years: to explore going into the ordained ministry. Certainly, the call of Christ was no less real to Bob than it was to the disciples in Jesus' day.

Responding to challenges and needs involves people at all places in their life spans. Children can be given careful encouragement to find tasks that use their gifts, time, and talents to participate in the response of the community of faith to various mission and service opportunities. We need to be asking how we can effectively and consistently help people experience the presence and power of Jesus Christ in their lives—wherever they are in their life spans—as they seek to respond to changes around them.

Application Questions

1. What are the factors that keep people in your community of faith from recognizing opportunities to serve?

2. Read Matthew 9:35–10:25. If Jesus were here today talking with you or your ministry group or council, how would he describe the mission to which he sends you?

3. Write down a simple, one-sentence prayer you could pray frequently to help with the discernment process. (Example: "O Spirit of Christ, let me be aware of my gifts and how I may meet the needs of others today.")

43

Participation in a Supportive Community

Tom and Susan Thompson were approached in August and asked to teach the fifth and sixth grade Sunday school class. They agreed to do so, were given the curriculum, and shown a small classroom where they would teach. The teacher guidelines spelled out the importance of being prepared and being in the classroom ten minutes before class began to meet the students. Susan and Tom approached their teaching with great dedication and seldom missed class. Unfortunately, their class met during the second service of worship, and it was often necessary to miss the first service entirely, in order to make last-minute preparations for the class.

The class went as well as could be expected, but by March the Thompsons were beginning to feel somewhat isolated. A good friend approached Susan and asked if they had been visiting another church, since she never saw them at fellowship time anymore. Susan felt a twinge of anger and sadness because she realized she was missing something she needed. Even though the teaching was satisfying and she knew how much the children needed their teaching, she realized that she was missing her weekly contact with some of her friends. Susan and Tom both knew they had been away from worship too much that year. The church had a recognition ritual for the Sunday school teachers in May at the first service. When the Sunday school superintendent asked if they would like to teach again the next year, they both responded without hesitation, "No, we just can't teach next year."

How frequently does this scenario repeat itself in our churches? It is fitting and appropriate to expect that people will make the commitment and sacrifice of time and effort to serve in different capacities, but we cannot expect them to do so on a regular basis without the support of community. For a wide variety of reasons, we take advantage of a person's willingness to serve. We do not make enough effort to make the task fit with what each person is able to do at that point in his or her life, and we fail to provide a supportive community in which the person can be involved. Later, we wonder why he or she gets burned out or drops out, or why no one responds when the church asks for volunteers.

As poignant as this situation is, it is only the tip of the iceberg when it comes to living as disciples throughout our lives. Tom and Susan needed to be part of a supportive small group, where they could work through the experiences they were having in the classroom, be held accountable in their spiritual journey, and to be shown appreciation for the use of their gifts. But they needed a supportive community even more as they attempted to live as disciples throughout the week.

No person should be asked to serve in any capacity within the life of the church, or on behalf of the church in service to others, without the church also providing a supportive community for that person. In a supportive community, the Spirit of Christ is present, people gather in a safe and respectful environment without judgment, and each person is given support and encouragement to carry out service and ministry in the church and in the world.

Whether people are serving on an ushering team, as part of the choir, as a kitchen helper, or with any other group in the church, they should experience these groups not just as task groups with a job to do but as places of supportive Christian community where they are able to grow in faith.

Application Questions

1. Ask each person to discuss, in small groups, how he or she has felt supported by the community of faith at critical times in his or her life.

2. Identify places in your community where better decision-making could happen if the people involved were surrounded by a supportive Christian community.

44

We must also pay attention to small groups, Bible study classes, support groups, and informal gatherings that provide ongoing supportive Christian community for people in their faith journeys. People can grow into deeper faith and discipleship if they are surrounded by community where the supportive presence of the Spirit of Christ is felt.

EXPERIENCES OF THE JOY OF SERVICE AND DISCIPLESHIP LEADING TO TRANSFORMATION OF LIFE

The story of Jesus raising Lazarus from the dead shows the transformation of life by those who put their whole trust and belief in Jesus the Messiah. Mary, Martha, and Lazarus were close friends of Jesus and were part of his supportive community. Three significant lessons emerge from this story.

The first lesson is to trust that the Holy Spirit will be present, will provide necessary guidance, and will likely surprise us. On the occasion when Lazarus was ill beyond the help of anyone else, Mary and Martha sent word to Jesus. They fully expected that Jesus would do great things. When Jesus arrived four days after Lazarus had been buried, Martha said, "Lord, if you had been here, my brother would not have died. But even now I know that God will give you whatever you ask of him" (John 11:21-22). Even though we trust that powerful things can happen when the Holy Spirit is invoked and trusted, we do not know what God ultimately may do. When Jesus told Martha that her brother would rise again, she thought he was referring to the future resurrection of the dead. But Jesus had something quite different in mind. He went into the tomb of the dead man and called him out; then Lazarus emerged alive.

Many times I have been part of a group working on a problem or issue. As we work together and open ourselves to the leading of God's Spirit, invariably some new solution becomes clear that none of us would have thought of on our own. It is the Spirit of Christ working in our midst that brings insight and new light to the situation. We must continually invite ourselves, and those with whom we work, to trust the presence and insights of the Spirit of Christ.

The second lesson that comes from this story is that we must roll away the stones that get in the way of transformation. When Jesus went to Lazarus' tomb, he said to the people there, "Take away the stone" (John 11:39). He could not bring Lazarus back to life unless the stone had been rolled away. Often, there are big stones in the way of our finding the right solution to a problem. We must listen to Jesus' words "Take away the stone." What are some of the stones that get in the way?

- Weariness and fatigue?
- Discouragement and frustration?
- Human failures?
- Not following through?
- Perceived lack of resources, knowledge, people power, and so forth?
- The common responses "We tried that, but it didn't work" or "We've never done it that way before"?

We must be willing to lay aside those things that are blocking us and let Jesus bring new insights and direction.

Now a certain man was ill, Lazarus of Bethany, the village of Mary and her sister Martha.... So the sisters sent a message to Jesus, "Lord, he whom you love is ill."... When Jesus arrived, he found that Lazarus had already been in the tomb four days.... Martha said to Jesus, "Lord, if you had been here, my brother would not have died. But even now I know that God will give you whatever you ask of him." Jesus said to her, "Your brother will rise again." Martha said to him, "I know that he will rise again in the resurrection on the last day." Jesus said to her, "I am the resurrection and the life. Those who believe in me, even though they die, will live, and everyone who lives and believes in me will never die. Do you believe this?" She said to him, "Yes, Lord, I believe that you are the Messiah, the Son of God, the one coming into the world."

(John 11:1-3, 17, 21-27)

45

Application Questions

1. In a small group where there is caring and understanding, discuss what it would be like to have Jesus join your group as an observer. What would he report concerning your process and time together?

2. What does it mean in your life to affirm, along with Martha, "Yes, Lord, I believe that you are the Messiah, the Son of God"?

The third lesson is this: Consider what Jesus said to Martha when they were talking: "I am the resurrection and the life. Those who believe in me, even though they die, will live, and everyone who lives and believes in me will never die." Then he asked Martha, "Do you believe this?" She said to him, "Yes, Lord, I believe that you are the Messiah, the Son of God, the one coming into the world" (John 11:25-27). Martha finally turned it all over to Jesus Christ and confessed her complete faith that he was the Messiah, the Son of God. Her faith and life were transformed from believing that Jesus could do marvelous things to knowing that he was the Messiah. As Jesus says to us, "Do you really believe this?" we can say along with Martha, "Yes, Lord, I believe that you are the Messiah, the Son of God, the one coming into the world." It is at this point that we enter into a deep and profound faith that transforms our lives. We realize that our lives are grounded in the heart of God, and we begin to see all of life from that perspective. We yearn for every opportunity to grow in this faith, to learn more about the way of life that Jesus taught and portrayed, and to let our life be refocused in new directions.

Chapter Seven

The Growing Points Star and the Means of Grace

Beginning relationship

Identifying gifts and responding to God's call

Integrating God's Word with life experiences

Experiencing Christian community

Supporting one another as we serve

When the day of Pentecost had come, they were all together in one place. And suddenly from heaven there came a sound like the rush of a violent wind, and it filled the entire house where they were sitting. Divided tongues, as of fire, appeared among them, and a tongue rested on each of them. All of them were filled with the Holy Spirit and began to speak in other languages, as the Spirit gave them ability.

(Acts 2:1-4)

Through experiences in the community of Christ, integrating God's Word with life experiences, the discovery and use of one's gifts, and participation in supportive community, a new reality begins to take shape. As our lives and spirits open up to the presence of God through Christ, we become aware of the breath of God filling our souls, and we begin to taste the realm of God as present reality. We have embarked on a journey of spiritual growth and discipleship that leads into ever-deepening levels of connection to the heart of God in Christ.

Through the Holy Spirit, God breathes new life and power into the person who is awakening to God's presence, just as the Holy Spirit brought new life to the disciples at Pentecost. Jesus told Nicodemus that this would happen:

For all who are led by the Spirit of God are children of God. For you did not receive a spirit of slavery to fall back into fear, but you have received a spirit of adoption. When we cry, "Abba! Father!" it is that very Spirit bearing witness with our spirit that we are children of God, and if children, then heirs, heirs of God and joint heirs with Christ—if, in fact, we suffer with him so that we may also be glorified with him.

(Romans 8:14-17)

Very truly, I tell you, no one can enter the kingdom of God without being born of water and Spirit.... Do not be astonished that I said to you, "You must be born from above." The wind blows where it chooses, and you hear the sound of it, but you do not know where it comes from or where it goes. So it is with everyone who is born of the Spirit.   (John 3:5-8)

All of the points on the Growing Points Star are important, and all have a role to play in helping people grow in Christian maturity; but at the center of the process is Christ. Essential to every point on the Star is the Spirit of Christ coming to life in us, growing from an initial spark to an ever-increasing center of light and power within our lives. We are growing toward Christ-likeness, a relationship in which our lives are joined with God's love, so that Christ is living in and through us. "It is no longer I who live, but it is Christ who lives in me," affirms Paul. "And the life I now live in the flesh I live by faith in the Son of God, who loved me and gave himself for me" (Galatians 2:20).

So, how do we grow toward Christ-likeness? John Wesley offered a model for growing into new levels of discipleship and faithfulness. Within his own life he practiced regular behaviors of the spirit and body, which led to deeper levels of faith and greater awareness of God's grace. He understood these to be means of grace, or channels through which we receive God's grace.

When discussing the various means of grace, Wesley often referred to works of piety and works of mercy. Works of piety included the public worship of God, family and private prayer, study of the Scriptures, the Lord's Supper, fasting or abstinence, and Christian conferencing or conversation. Works of mercy included things such as visiting the sick and those in prison, feeding the hungry, and clothing the poor.

John Wesley also made it clear that all outward activities, if separate from the Spirit of God, cannot produce in any degree either the knowledge or love of God. No inherent power exists in the words that are spoken in prayer, in the Scripture that is read, or in the bread and wine received in the Lord's Supper; "but that it is God alone who is the Giver of every good gift, the Author of all grace" (from Wesley's sermon "The Means of Grace").

In many ways, the means of grace are like navigation tools that keep the ship on course; they keep our spirits centered in God's Spirit. The various means of grace keep us connected to Christ, the center for all of the growing points.

As spiritual leaders, we must practice the means of grace. We must help others develop spiritual disciplines to avail their spirits to means through which God can become known to them. At the same time, we need to be hearing Wesley's reminder that God may choose at any time to grant the gift of grace, even though no means have been observed.

Although some means of grace seem to relate more closely to one growing point or another, they really are at the center of the Star and can be tied to all of the growing points.

1. PERSONAL DEVOTION THROUGH SCRIPTURE AND PRAYER

Through personal efforts to connect with God, such as Scripture, devotional literature, and private prayer, one experiences the beginning relationship with God over and over again. Daily devotions are a way of saying "hello" to God, just as one interacts with one's closest, most intimate friends. But through prayer and daily reflection on the Scripture, we relate to God in a far deeper manner than we relate to our friends. As prayer and the study of the Scriptures are engaged in together, each informs and strengthens the other. Praying the Scriptures is the understanding that God is present in the words of the text and is speaking directly to us in our current circumstances.

Scripture

Upon completing a DISCIPLE Bible study class, Mark told the congregation, "Studying the Bible every day over these months has brought a whole new purpose to my life. I feel much closer to God now and can take things in stride at work." Through Scripture study, our relationship with Christ is strengthened, and we are able to integrate the biblical story with our own life experiences.

John Wesley found in the Scripture both a sense of direction and a source of spiritual food. People who learn to receive the word of God daily through Scripture also receive the fresh and empowering breath of God in their daily lives. But our need for daily input from God's Word goes beyond just our personal lives. We must also look critically at the lack of attention given to the Scriptures in our households and families. What would it mean for Christian people to revive such customs of earlier years as reading the Bible daily at mealtime as a family or household?

It is important to develop the regular routine and practice of daily interaction with God's Word as a means of receiving and living with God's grace. Many resources are available to assist both individuals and families with the discipline of daily Scripture reading, study, and reflection.

Daily Prayer

Prayer is the means of receiving the breath of God, which brings us life beyond the surface life of physical existence. Prayer is the soul's sincere desire and is the way of being assured that "God knows my name and cares about me." Daily practices of prayer and meditation lead to a life that is more consistently in tune with God's will.

John Wesley frequently talked about "family prayer," suggesting that having everyone in the household gather for prayer and devotions is of value. One day, eight-year-old Jaque told his Sunday school teacher, "I like it when my family prays the Lord's Prayer together. It feels just right." Although he may not have used theological language to express himself, Jaque had experienced family communal prayer as a means of grace. We can encourage families to pray at mealtimes and to develop other patterns for regular family prayer and devotions.

It is not the intention of this book to explore all of the facets of developing a daily prayer life, but rather to call attention to the importance of daily prayer in our lives. When we, as spiritual leaders, learn within our own lives the importance of daily prayer, we cannot help but share with others our convictions and insights of its importance.

Intercessory Prayer

As one grows in faith and discipleship, the sense of being connected in community expands to an awareness of belonging to God's creation and caring for all God's children throughout the world. It is generally too much to

All scripture is inspired by God and is useful for teaching, for reproof, for correction, and for training in righteousness, so that everyone who belongs to God may be proficient, equipped for every good work.

(2 Timothy 3:16-17)

My mouth will tell of your righteous acts, of your deeds of salvation all day long, though their number is past my knowledge. I will come praising the mighty deeds of the Lord GOD. I will praise your righteousness, yours alone.

(Psalm 71:15-16)

49

O God, you are my God, I seek you, my soul thirsts for you; my flesh faints for you, as in a dry and weary land where there is no water. So I have looked upon you in the sanctuary, beholding your power and glory. Because your steadfast love is better than life, my lips will praise you. So I will bless you as long as I live; I will lift up my hands and call on your name.

(Psalm 63:1-4)

Application Questions

1. Examine carefully your own practices of personal prayer and study of the Scriptures. Keep track of how consistently you adhere to daily prayer. Determine how you can adjust your daily routine to allow regular time for prayer and Scripture.

2. Make a list of opportunities that you have to tell others about the values and importance of the practice of daily prayer and Scripture.

50

comprehend all God's children at once. Thus, those in need who enter one's consciousness and concern at any one time make up the "community of the world" of which one is a part.

Such broader community does not replace the smaller supportive community in which one participates, but it becomes a wider sphere of connection. It manifests itself as a prayer community, characterized by one's daily prayer for others, by one's lifting the needs of others in thought and story as one goes about daily life, and possibly by engaging in acts of compassion and justice to benefit those about whom one is concerned.

Just as with every other aspect of a growing faith, reaching out to others in compassion and prayer also draws life, energy, and inspiration from the presence of Jesus Christ. As we grow in our response to others and feel connected to the needs of God's children, it is in reality the Spirit of Christ growing within us and connecting us with God's love and compassion for all.

2. Gathering in the Name of Christ: Christian Fellowship

When John Wesley talked about Christian fellowship, he was not referring to a gathering of people with refreshments and light conversation. Rather, he understood the marks of Christian fellowship to be watching over one another in love, praying for one another, holding one another accountable for growth in discipleship, and discussing with one another our spiritual joys and challenges.

Being drawn into a small group in which the Spirit of Christ is consciously present is an invaluable introduction to true Christian community. The depth and significance of small-group community is increasingly important for new Christians. As trust develops within the group, members are usually more willing to reveal areas in their life where spiritual growth or challenges are occurring. As this happens, the growing Christian senses deeper commitment toward other members of the group and toward the group itself, and Christian fellowship occurs. Christian fellowship is closely related to both the welcoming community of the second growing point and the supportive community of the fifth growing point.

The early Methodists understood the importance of small groups for the development of discipleship; therefore, they divided into small groups called classes. The members of the classes held one another accountable for their discipleship, as described in the General Rules: do no harm, do good (acts of mercy), participate in the ordinances of God (acts of piety).

Covenant Discipleship Groups of today are based on the principles of the early Methodist class meetings. Small groups meet weekly to hold one another accountable as disciples. Each group develops a covenant to guide their discipleship, which includes regular participation in both works of piety and works of mercy. Through mutual support and accountability, they watch over one another in love.

People in DISCIPLE Bible study groups all around the world have discovered this aspect of the Christian life. They initially come together to engage in intensive Bible study, agreeing to the daily Bible readings, reflection, and the weekly meeting of two and a half hours. But week by week, as the members of the group study, share, and work with each other, they sense a growing connection and the joy of being together.

Some youth who are serious about growing in their faith gather early one morning a week for a simple breakfast and Bible study and to encourage one another to be engaged in daily reading of the Scriptures. Many such groups have found that such meetings provide a refreshing surge of spiritual energy and wisdom in the middle of the week.

In some churches where worship is creative and responsive to God's Word, and where the community has a sense of gathering in the presence of the Holy Spirit, worship itself may provide a regular opportunity for Christian fellowship. This is especially true in small-membership churches.

As district superintendent of the Northwest District in Minnesota, I was keenly aware that eight or ten small rural churches in the district functioned as this type of community. One was a church with twelve members and an average Sunday worship attendance of thirteen to fourteen—almost always the same group of people, who described themselves as "the gathering of the people of Christ of our area." Another was a rural congregation that in six years grew from an average worship attendance of thirty to nearly one hundred, "because [they] let God's Spirit become [their] guide for everything that [they] do."

Application Questions

1. Describe your own experiences of Christian fellowship.

2. Describe some steps you could take to make Christian fellowship a reality in a group in which you participate.

3. Gathering for Worship: Word and Sacrament

Discovering our story in the midst of God's story is at the heart of the third growing point. Especially within worship—but also at any time when we reflect on the various events in our lives and find ourselves surrounded by and immersed in passages of Scripture—we are being drawn into God's story made known to us through the Scriptures. One of the means of grace identified by John Wesley was to hear the Word preached or proclaimed regularly. His practice of preaching an average of two to three times daily for more than forty years bears testimony to the importance he gave to preaching and hearing the Word proclaimed. Actually, for Wesley, receiving God's Word as a means of grace included having it read, heard, preached, and meditated upon. We must reluctantly acknowledge that for some people, attending worship with the gathered community on a weekly basis provides the only opportunity for the Word to be brought into their lives. Thus, we must do all we can to make this as effective a means of grace as possible.

Being drawn into God's story happens in no greater depth than when participating in the sacraments of baptism and Holy Communion. Observing the sacraments was an important means of grace for John Wesley. Baptism is the sacrament that welcomes us into the family of God. The baptismal ritual and the ritual for the renewal of the Baptismal Covenant provide continual reminders of our calling to discipleship through baptism.

In the closing episode of the story of the disciples meeting Christ on the road to Emmaus, we read that although Jesus had been walking with the disciples for some distance, had interpreted the Scriptures, and had spoken with them about what they had just experienced in Jerusalem, they did not recognize him as Jesus Christ. The recognition did not occur until he sat with them at the table and blessed and broke the bread (Luke 24:13-31). This story points out how important it is for us to participate regularly in the Lord's Supper as a means of grace. Joining with others at the table of Holy Communion has the potential of being the catalyst that allows one to experience the presence of the risen Christ. As the events in the life of Jesus are recalled, the words Jesus spoke

When he was at the table with them, he took bread, blessed and broke it, and gave it to them. Then their eyes were opened, and they recognized him.

(Luke 24:30-31)

51

Application Questions

1. Reflect on your congregation's services of worship. Then decide what can be done to help them become a more effective means of grace.

2. How is the sacrament of Holy Communion a means of grace for you?

Therefore, since we are justified by faith, we have peace with God through our Lord Jesus Christ, through whom we have obtained access to this grace in which we stand; and we boast in our hope of sharing the glory of God. And not only that, but we also boast in our sufferings, knowing that suffering produces endurance, and endurance produces character, and character produces hope, and hope does not disappoint us, because God's love has been poured into our hearts through the Holy Spirit that has been given to us. (Romans 5:1-5)

at the Last Supper are recounted, and the bread and cup are shared, people experience the presence of Christ and the assurance of new life. We receive the power and strength of the Holy Spirit and are filled with new hope and possibilities for living as more-faithful disciples. It is no wonder that John Wesley felt that every Christian should participate in the sacrament of the Lord's Supper as often as possible.

4. Doing Good: Acts of Mercy

The overarching theme of Jesus' teaching, healing, and work among the people was a compelling drive and compassion to care for all people in need. For Jesus, following God's commandments meant loving God with all one's heart, soul, and mind, and loving one's neighbor as one's self (Mark 12:29-31). Jesus spoke about being the "salt of the earth" and letting one's light shine, rather than hiding it under a bushel basket, so that others can see one's good works and glorify God in heaven (Matthew 5:13-16). When it came time to send his disciples out, Jesus gave them "power and authority over all demons and to cure diseases" and told them to "proclaim the kingdom of God and to heal" (Luke 9:1-2).

Feeling and responding to God's call requires an openness and readiness to let one's gifts unfold and be used in response to needs in the world. Discovering one's gifts and being called into service becomes a direct avenue for experiencing God's grace and outpouring of love. As we reach out to the needs elsewhere in God's creation, we are able not only to make a positive difference but also to become the means by which the compassion of Christ touches the brokenness of the world, bringing justice and redemption. This is the theme of the fourth growing point as it unfolds in a lifetime of discipleship.

After the Red River of the North overran its banks in the spring of 1997 and flooded the communities in its path, thousands of people fearfully returned to their homes to see if anything was left. The hundreds of work teams and thousands of individuals who responded over a two-year period to help with the rebuilding process brought much more than their labors and skills; they brought hope and faith in God's renewing, re-creating love.

Water filled the basement of Joe's home up to the first floor. He was not a particularly religious man, but he recalls that as he stepped back into the house, feeling overwhelmed with discouragement and uncertainty, he looked for some sign that he could depend on God. After pumping water out of the basement down to several feet, he walked down to survey the damage. Looking into the room where his library had been, he saw hundreds of books bulging with water floating on the water. But the book closest to him did not seem to be water-damaged, even though it was floating on the water. He picked it up and saw that it was his Bible. He said as he fought back tears, "The first book that came to me out of that whole mess was my Bible. It was not soaked up with water like the rest, so I knew that God would see us through this. You folks, and all the others who have come, have helped me get back on my feet. I will never doubt God again!" What Joe did not realize was that by telling his story to each group that came to help him, he was reinforcing the role played by the Spirit of Christ to affirm the gifts being shared by others and their involvement in acts of compassion and justice.

Some congregations are learning how to make service and mission an ongoing part of their identity and ministry. The issue at stake is how to order our life as the body of Christ in such a way that carrying out acts of compassion and justice is part of the definition of who we are. In order to make disciples, we must first be disciples sent to proclaim that the kingdom of God is at hand.

Summary

The means of grace ground us in a life that sustains our faith in God and our relationship with Christ, ensuring that we continue to live and serve as disciples in the world. Furthermore, it undergirds our role as spiritual leaders in a church that seeks to be the body of Christ in the world.

Application Questions

1. Describe the ways in which you engage in acts of mercy. How do these experiences help you grow spiritually?

2. Identify which groups in your community of faith could be responsible for encouraging others to be involved in acts of mercy.

Using the Growing Points Star

Chapter Eight

Beginning relationship

Identifying gifts and
responding to God's call

Integrating God's Word
with life experiences

Experiencing Christian
community

Supporting one
another as we serve

Listen! I am standing at the door, knocking; if you hear my voice and
open the door, I will come in to you and eat with you, and you with me.
(Revelation 3:20)

Working with the Growing Points Star means consistently
recognizing and paying attention to five basic arenas in
which new faith in Christ is formed or deeper faith in Jesus Christ is
encouraged. Emphasizing the points does not draw the focus away from the
presence of Jesus Christ at the center of the Star; rather, the points draw life
and energy from the One at the center.

Jesus Christ stands at the door of our hearts, gently knocking. In one
hand he holds a lantern to bring light to the darkness around us. As people
of faith, we know that he leads the way to a transformed life and offers the
invitation to live as disciples. What we must also recognize, and what we
must take seriously, is that the effectiveness of the environment surrounding
each of the growing points depends on us.

As the church, we need to identify and work consistently with factors
that facilitate one's pathway to Christ. As the body of Christ and as
Christian community, we can pay closer attention to the arenas covered by

Therefore prepare your minds for action; discipline yourselves; set all your hope on the grace that Jesus Christ will bring you when he is revealed.... Through him you have come to trust in God, who raised him from the dead and gave him glory, so that your faith and hope are set on God.

(1 Peter 1:13, 21)

the growing points. It has little to do with the size of the congregation. What is required in all settings is spiritual leaders who intentionally take responsibility for the dynamics relating to the growing points in the following ways.

1. Understanding the Growing Points

Leaders who want to have a positive impact on the developing faith of others will learn about the factors that influence developing faith and will work to ensure that these elements are consistently cared for by the community of faith.

When a group of leaders gathered to explore the dynamics that lead to new and developing faith, a variety of experiences were discussed. Several people mentioned that in a camp or retreat setting the environment, the people gathered, and the community that is created can combine to create a powerful opportunity for growth in faith. A person who had been involved in leading worship for seekers discussed the importance of being sensitive to where people are in their life experiences as they come to the service. Someone else with significant background in short-term mission work spoke about the importance of helping people recognize and use their gifts. A participant in a Covenant Discipleship Group witnessed to the importance of small-group support and accountability. Together, they all recognized that each of the aspects mentioned contributes to the whole. No one element stands alone, and the whole is not complete without attention being given to the contribution made by each part.

2. Practicing the Means of Grace

The spiritual disciplines covered in the previous chapters are time-honored, well-accepted practices that lead to deeper faith and a closer relationship with Jesus Christ. People who become spiritual leaders start out as people who take seriously their own spiritual journeys. They develop personal spiritual disciplines that become means of learning about and receiving God's redeeming grace. They become spiritual leaders as Jesus Christ touches their lives in the way that he touched the lives of the disciples and others around him, and in the same way he has touched the lives of followers ever since. They become spiritual leaders as they respond to the touch of Christ on their lives, find their story in God's story, discover their gifts, and reach out to others. They become spiritual leaders as Christ lives in them and reaches out to others through their thoughts, actions, and leadership. Spiritual leaders are ordinary people who let Christ do extraordinary things in their lives.

3. Being Aware of Where Others Are in Their Faith Journeys

Spiritual leaders are consciously aware of others around them in the journey of faith. Just as a good leader on a hike is always aware of the other hikers' needs and makes sure that they are coming along, so the spiritual leader is sensitive to where others are in their journeys of faith. Good leaders take initiative to listen to the people they are leading, to teach in appropriate ways, to coach when necessary, and to lead others in understanding the factors that contribute to a developing faith in Jesus Christ.

In whatever group or setting they find themselves, spiritual leaders take every opportunity to call attention to the main work of the body of Christ, which is to make disciples who live in a way that transforms the world around them so that the kingdom of God can be realized. The main flow or direction of all our activity, as inspired and empowered by the Holy Spirit, is to raise up people who know Jesus Christ and desire to live as faithful disciples. We must do this unabashedly and without apologies, for no other activity or work is more important for the church to be doing.

If people are living as faithful disciples, they will see to it that all other aspects necessary for the life of the Body are cared for, and that the Body is about the ministry of Christ in the world. But first and foremost, attention must always be given to helping people come to know Jesus Christ and grow in faith as his followers. Spiritual leaders will see that this is always given top priority. One of the ways to do this is to consistently call attention to the growing points and the ways Christ is present in those points.

4. Helping Others Know Christ

The early disciples had a burning passion for sharing their faith in Jesus Christ and were willing to face persecution, go to prison, and lose their lives in order to do this. What has happened to our passion for sharing our faith in Christ? What the body of Christ needs now, in the twenty-first century, is people who will help others come to know Christ and grow in faith. We need parents and grandparents and church members who want their children and youth to learn about Jesus Christ and who are willing to do what it takes to help them grow in faith. We need people who want to share their faith with others who are living with no awareness of God's love. We need churches that will focus everything they are doing to help people meet Jesus Christ, grow in the faith, and live as disciples.

5. Being Channels of the Holy Spirit

A small group of people met with their district superintendent to ask what could be done to save their dying church. After getting all the facts on the table and exploring many scenarios, the superintendent finally said, "I have no answers. Only God knows what needs to happen for this church in this community. The one thing you can do, if you really want the right answer, is to continue to meet every week, read the Scriptures, and pray for God's Spirit to lead the way." When the superintendent returned on a Sunday morning six months later, the worship was much the same as it had been. However, several women in the group said with excitement, "We haven't gotten any answers yet, but we are having a wonderful prayer fellowship, and some new people from the community have even joined us. We are finding God again!" With this beginning, the church began to grow and find new life.

God can and will do marvelous things when we give God a chance. But it takes spiritual leadership to call attention to what God can do and to keep the focus on being open to the presence of Christ, who is the head of the Body. It takes leadership to invite the Body to hear God's Word, to study it, and to pray for guidance. It takes leadership to trust that the Holy Spirit will give guidance, insight, and power.

Using the Growing Points Star

As a Means for Personal Growth and Understanding

Look at the first growing point, beginning relationship, and remember your own beginnings in the faith. How did you first experience Jesus Christ? Where were you? Who were the other people involved in the experience? Did you first receive the gentle touch of Christ's love through the action of another, or did your first experience with Christ come as a private experience, either quietly or like a lightning bolt in the night?

As you move to each of the other growing points, think about your own experience and recall how you have grown in your relationship with Christ through the elements of each point. You may also think of the stories of other people that help to illustrate each growing point.

As a Way to Help Others Reflect on Their Faith Journeys

The light of Christ really begins to glow when you are exploring the growing points with others and become a coach to others as they take steps leading to new faith. This may be done by covering all five growing points in one session, or by having a session for each of the growing points. Use drawings on newsprint or overhead transparencies to show each growing point. The diagram on page 62 can be used to make transparencies. Make a separate transparency for each growing point. Give personal examples or illustrations. Then invite the group to tell about their reflections on each point.

It is important to recognize that while there is a logical progression in the flow from growing point one through growing point five, they do not illustrate a linear process. People may enter the Star at any point. For example, youth participating in a work camp may first discover Christ's love as they share their skills, time, and resources with someone in need. Later, as they reflect on the experience, they may begin to discover the joys of the other growing points.

As an Evaluation Tool

Once the group has learned about all five points, they can move to a careful analysis of the effectiveness of ministry in various areas. Consider using the following evaluation process.
1. Give each participant a photocopy of the Growing Points Star (page 63).
2. Select one area in the life of the church to examine (for example, Sunday morning worship, a youth program, choir, an outreach ministry, and so forth).
3. Ask each individual to consider the area identified in Step 2 in relationship to each of the growing points, asking: *How well is this working for me? for other participants? for newcomers?*
4. Lead the group in a discussion about the previous step, moving fairly quickly from one growing point to the next. For each point, have the group decide how they would rate the area being evaluated. Then place a check mark on the dotted line. The farther the check mark is from the center of the Star, the better the group believes they are doing. Connect the check marks with lines to create a new Star within the Star on the photocopy. The check marks become the end points of the new Star. This shows a picture of your current effectiveness related to the five areas of faith growth addressed by the growing points.

5. Then for each point place an *X* on the dotted line where the group would like to be in order to more effectively help people come to know Jesus Christ and grow in their faith. Join the *X's* to form another Star. This represents the group's goal for helping to increase effectiveness.
6. Have the group divide into pairs or small groups. Assign each group one of the points of the Star, and ask them to think of two or three ideas that would help move the check mark closer to the *X*. Have each group report back to the larger group.
7. Develop a plan or strategy for accomplishing at least one of the goals leading to each point of the Star, emphasizing the points identified as needing the most attention. Set a time to evaluate how the goal is progressing.

As a Guide for Preaching and Worship

The weekly service of worship is the greatest opportunity congregations have to reach the largest number of people in matters that have to do with the faith. It stands to reason that we want every aspect surrounding that experience (planning, greeting, ushering, preaching, singing, and so forth) to be done with an eye toward helping people meet God through Jesus Christ, grow in their faith, and be encouraged to live as disciples.

The five growing points identify areas that should be given careful attention as we oversee the worship life of the congregation. Taking the worship service as a whole, there must be an appropriate balance between all five points of the Star. When one or more aspects are given less attention, the potential of reaching every person in a way that will contribute to their faith journey is diminished. The person relatively new to faith in Christ must experience the initial aspects of being drawn into community where the Spirit of Christ is felt. The person searching for meaning must hear God's story in a way that connects to his or her own personal story and helps him or her to feel valued as a child of God with gifts to offer. The person engaged in service must feel the support of the larger community of faith and the encouragement to continue in the face of struggle and discouragement. We all must worship with an expectant spirit, knowing that the Holy Spirit is present, giving inspiration, guidance, and power. When the person preaching is consciously aware of the growing points, he or she can be more intentional about including these elements in the sermon.

The United Methodist Basic Pattern of Worship is described on pages 2–5 in *The United Methodist Hymnal* and on pages 13–32 in *The United Methodist Book of Worship*. As we plan each movement of the worship service (Entrance, Proclamation and Response, Thanksgiving and Communion, and Sending Forth), we need to consider how the growing points are expressed. Do those who are beginning a relationship with Christ feel safe and welcome throughout the service? Do all worshipers have an experience of Christian community? Do the worshipers encounter God and one another through the music, prayers, proclamation of Scripture, and Holy Communion? Does the worship service provide opportunities to respond to God's call? Do the worshipers leave the service as people who are sent into the world as Christ's disciples? For example, one congregation has discovered that it is helpful to include a "mission moment" just prior to the closing hymn as a way of recognizing and supporting those who are in service. During this time each week, one person is invited to tell about some aspect of his or her life as a disciple of Christ. The entire congregation increases their awareness of supporting one another in faithful living as disciples.

Using the growing points in worship is not intended to be yet another theory of what should happen in worship, but rather it should complement a full and complete understanding of worship planning and leadership.

As a Way to Help Refocus Organizational Functions

The 1996 General Conference of The United Methodist Church took many steps to shift the focus of local church administration from that of doing maintenance and administration to that of being engaged in ministry and mission. The challenge for us in our areas of ministry is to shift the focus and mindset of much of our activity in churches from doing administration and maintaining our buildings and programs to being engaged in ministry and mission where people can experience the presence of Christ and be held accountable for living the life of discipleship.

Paying attention to the growing points can help to make this shift. Present an overview of the Growing Points Star to the church council or a gathering of key leaders of the church. It is best to resist the temptation of dividing up the growing points to present at different times, since they all must be seen as parts of the whole, with Christ at the center. You may want to prepare an overhead transparency of the Growing Points Star, using the diagram (page 62). Become familiar enough with each growing point so that you can speak from your own experience and understanding. Allow time for discussion of each growing point, and engage the group in serious discussion about what changes may need to be made in order to draw sharper attention to the growing points.

All groups and ministry teams need to focus their attention on forming disciples. This transformation is needed not only by church councils but also by boards of trustees, finance committees, and every other group that meets within the life of the church. In fact, there is no group that meets or any task performed that is so important that the task overshadows faith formation. Being the body of Christ means that Christ is the head; Christ is present; and our purpose for being is to live out the life of the Body: doing the work of Christ in the world.

How would our church meetings be different if we replaced the ordinary opening prayer with a twenty-minute serious study of an appropriate passage of Scripture? I use this process regularly, in spite of the reluctant people who say, "Let's get down to the real business for which we are here." I let them know that hearing God's Word and finding out what God wants us to be doing is precisely why we are here. We have no business doing anything as the body of Christ if we do not invite the Spirit of Christ to be present in our meetings.

A helpful exercise for the church council or a leadership team is to study Ephesians 4:1-6, 11-16. In small groups, study the various sections in relation to your own church. How do Paul's suggestions relate to your situation? How could you take this passage more seriously as a congregation?

CLOSING

As one becomes aware of the touch of Christ's love, experiences the presence of Christ in community, becomes immersed in God's story, discovers gifts that are called into service, and becomes involved in supportive Christian community, Christ becomes an increasingly real presence. All of life is transformed into a new way of knowing one's self in relation to God and the world. The desire to live this new reality molds and shapes everything that one is and does. This is the life of discipleship.

I close with the prayer that in discovering growing points for your faith, you have gained new insights about your faith journey. I pray that the love and light coming from Christ at the center will illumine your life so that at any moment you find yourself immersed in the richness of God's love, a love that will draw you in and transform the world around you.

Growing Points Star

Beginning relationship

I hear my name

Identifying gifts and responding to God's call

Integrating God's Word with life experiences

I am called

I experience God

I belong here

I walk with others

Experiencing Christian community

Supporting one another as we serve

© 2000 Discipleship Resources. Permission is granted to the purchaser of *The Growing Points Star* to reproduce this page for local church use.

Growing Points Star

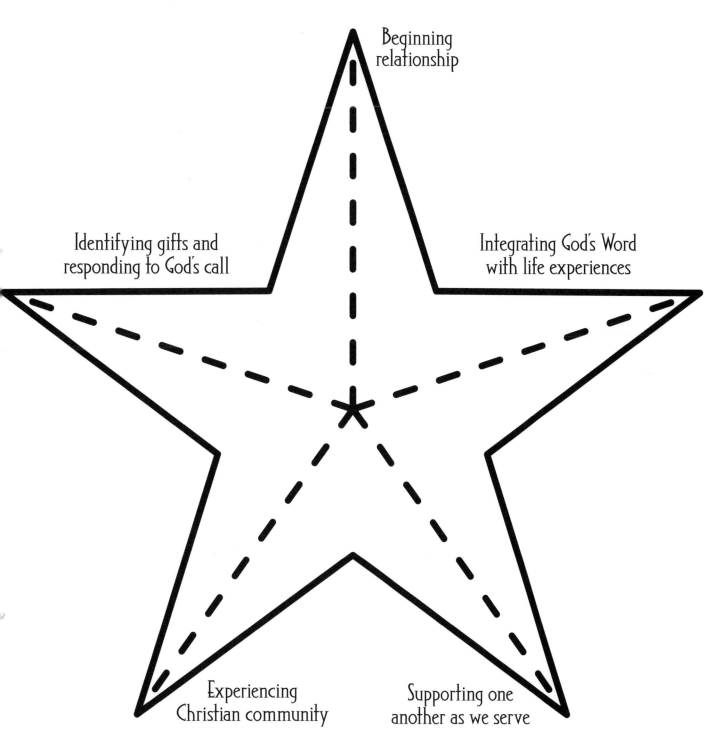

Beginning
relationship

Identifying gifts and
responding to God's call

Integrating God's Word
with life experiences

Experiencing
Christian community

Supporting one
another as we serve

© 2000 Discipleship Resources. Permission is granted to the purchaser of *The Growing Points Star* to reproduce this page for local church use.